RAND

1700 Main Street, PO Box 2138 Santa Monica, CA 90407-2138

ERRATUM

May 30, 1997

To: Recipient of MR-836-NCRVE/UCB

Title: Using Alternative Assessments in Vocational Education

Authors: Brian M. Stecher, Mikala L. Rahn, Allen Ruby, Martha Naomi Alt, Abby Robyn

Please note that there are two errors on page ii ("Funding Information"). The Grant Number should read: V051A30003-95A/V051A30004-95A. The sixth item, "Director," is David Stern.

We apologize for any confusion.

National Center for Research in Vocational Education
University of California, Berkeley

Using Alternative Assessments in Vocational Education

Brian M. Stecher
Mikala L. Rahn
Allen Ruby
Martha Naomi Alt
Abby Robyn

with
Brian Ward

Supported by
the Office of Vocational and Adult Education
U.S. Department of Education

FUNDING INFORMATION

Project Title: National Center for Research in Vocational Education

Grant Number: V051A30004-93A/V051A30003-93A

Act Under Which   Carl D. Perkins Vocational Education Act
Funds Administered: P.L. 98-524

Source of Grant: Office of Vocational and Adult Education
U.S. Department of Education
Washington, D.C. 20202

Grantee: The Regents of the University of California
c/o National Center for Research in Vocational
   Education
2030 Addison St., Suite 500
Berkeley, CA 94720-1674

Director: Charles S. Benson

Percent of Total
Grant Financed by
Federal Money: 100%

Dollar Amount
of Federal Funds
for Grant: $6,000,000

Disclaimer: This publication was prepared pursuant to a grant with the Office of Vocational and Adult Education, U.S. Department of Education. Grantees undertaking such projects under government sponsorship are encouraged to express freely their judgment in professional and technical matters. Points of view or opinions do not, therefore, necessarily represent official U.S. Department of Education position or policy.

Discrimination: Title VI of the Civil Rights Act of 1964 states: "No person in the United States shall, on the ground of race, color, or national origin, be excluded from participation in, be denied the benefits of, or be subjected to discrimination under any program or activity receiving federal financial assistance." Title IX of the Education Amendments of 1972 states: "No person in the United States shall, on the basis of sex, be excluded from participation in, be denied the benefits of, or be subjected to discrimination under any education program or activity receiving federal financial assistance." Therefore, the National Center for Research in Vocational Education project, like every program or activity receiving financial assistance from the U.S. Department of Education, must be operated in compliance with these laws.

Student assessment has always played an important role in vocational education, and recent changes in assessment practices may hold great promise for vocational educators. A RAND study was conducted to examine alternative forms of assessment from the perspective of vocational educators. Two products resulted. The first is this report, which describes a variety of assessment alternatives, reviews examples from extended case studies, and discusses criteria for choosing among the alternatives. This report should be of interest to vocational educators at the state and local level, particularly those responsible for decisions about the form and use of assessment systems. The second product is a set of training materials to help vocational educators make effective decisions about assessments. These materials are to be offered as a supplement to *Getting to Work: A Guide for Better Schools* (Rahn et al., 1995), a recent National Center for Research in Vocational Education (NCRVE) training package.

CONTENTS

FIGURES

The purpose of this study was to evaluate the utility of nontraditional forms of assessment for vocational education. This issue is particularly important at the present time because both vocational education and educational assessment are undergoing significant changes. In education, enrollment in high school vocational courses is dropping, the nature of vocational students is changing, and employers are calling for applicants who possess skills different from those of the past. In assessment, new forms of constructed-response measures, including performance tasks, portfolios, and senior projects, are gaining popularity, and assessment is being used more prominently as a policy tool. The confluence of these factors makes this an opportune time to take a careful look at the potential value of alternative forms of assessment for vocational education.

For our study, which ran from 1994 to 1996, we selected six cases that reflected a wide range of assessment options, with particular emphasis on operational programs using constructed-response measures. In each case, we conducted a critical review of the assessment system based on descriptive materials provided by the program, research literature, telephone interviews, and, in all but two cases, a one- to two-day site visit. Our investigations focused on program definition, implementation, and administration; the quality and feasibility of the assessments; and the potential usefulness of the assessment approach for vocational educators. Most, but not all, of our cases were drawn from vocational education. They include the Career-Technical Assessment Program, the Kentucky Instructional Results Information System, the Laborers-Associated General Contractors environmental training and certification programs, the

National Board for Professional Teaching Standards certification program, the Oklahoma Department of Vocational-Technical Education competency-based testing program, and the Vocational/ Industrial Clubs of America national competition.

By comparing these assessment systems, we were able to identify a number of important design and implementation considerations that should inform decisions about the use of alternative assessments in vocational education (and, more broadly, assessment planning in any educational context). First, the user must clarify the purpose of the assessment because the intended use (e.g., improving learning and instruction, certifying mastery) affects the choice of assessment method. Second, the user must understand the nature of the skills being assessed. Different cognitive demands (e.g., factual knowledge, integrated problem solving) may be better measured with one type of assessment than with another. Third, the user should become familiar with the range of alternative assessment options available. We identify four categories of assessments that may be of interest to vocational educators: written assessments, portfolios, performance tasks, and senior projects. Fourth, the user should understand the advantages and disadvantages of each assessment strategy. We describe several dimensions along which alternative assessments may differ, the two most important being quality (which includes reliability, validity, and fairness) and feasibility (which includes cost, time, complexity, and credibility). We discuss the quality and feasibility of the assessment types identified. Fifth, the user should be aware of certain other issues involved in designing assessment systems that might be relevant to a particular program or setting. We review the relative advantages of single versus multiple measures, low versus high stakes, standardization versus adaptability, embedded versus stand-alone assessments, single versus multiple purposes, and voluntary versus mandatory participation.

Finally, we illustrate how vocational educators can use this review to think about the usefulness of alternative assessments for a particular situation. We describe a procedure for evaluating the utility of alternative assessments that includes analyzing the purposes of the assessment and the skills to be assessed, considering alternative types of assessment, reviewing their quality and feasibility, and considering other factors identified in the case studies. This approach is illustrated by two scenarios that describe assessment problems faced by vocational educators and show how the results of this study can contribute to their resolution.

ACKNOWLEDGMENTS

The initial framework for this study was extremely broad, as was the list of operational assessment programs we might investigate. Fortunately, the members of our advisory committee helped us narrow our focus and select an interesting set of assessment case studies. For this help we are grateful to Charles Hopkins, Oklahoma Department of Education; Harry O'Neil, University of Southern California; Dean Petersen, Glendale Union High School District; Stanley Rabinowitz, WestEd; Catherine B. Smith, Michigan Department of Education; and Jonathan Troper, Center for Research on Evaluation, Standards, and Student Testing, UCLA. We wish to thank the program administrators, teachers, participants, and researchers who responded to our interview questions as part of the case studies of the Career-Technical Assessment Program, the Kentucky Instructional Results Information System, the Laborers-Associated General Contractors environmental training and certification programs, the National Board for Professional Teaching Standards certification program, the Oklahoma Department of Vocational-Technical Education competency-based testing program, and the Vocational/Industrial Clubs of America national competition. In addition, our thanks go to many other staff from testing and assessment projects who helped us gather information in our initial investigations of operational alternative assessments. Finally, credit is due to David Adamson and Jeri O'Donnell for their efforts to improve the clarity of this report and to Judy Wood and Donna White for their help with document preparation.

Chapter One

INTRODUCTION

During the past few years, economic concerns have prompted a number of proposals aimed at reforming federal vocational education and employment training programs. Reports about the inadequate skills of high school graduates, the rapidly changing demands of the workplace, and the declining competitiveness of U.S. firms in the international marketplace have all fueled the idea that the organization and structure of employment preparation programs must change. The 104th Congress argued at length about this issue, but Democrats and Republicans were not able to reach a consensus about the shape of future federal vocational education programs.

However, despite the strong differences in their approaches to reform, all sides seem to agree on the need for trustworthy methods for assessing vocational students' skills. A noteworthy example of this convergence can be seen in the continuing debate between those who recommend a greater focus on broad, industry skills at the secondary level (Boesel and McFarland, 1994) and those who place more emphasis on occupation-specific skills (Bishop, 1995). Both sides agree about the need for a system that assesses skills in reliable and valid ways. Almost all policy makers think it is essential to measure the degree to which participants have mastered the skills upon which training focuses.

Moreover, many vocational educators are advocating the wider use of alternative assessments, such as portfolios, exhibitions, and performance events, for measuring skills of either type. This interest in new measures derives in part from the changes occurring in vocational education. Educators and employers believe that the work world is changing and vocational education must adapt if it is to serve students well. The changes in the workplace are complex and not completely understood, but most observers believe that future employees will need integrated academic and vocational knowledge, a broad understanding of occupational areas, the ability to interact creatively with their peers, and higher-order cognitive skills that allow them to be flexible, learn rapidly, and adapt to ever-changing circumstances. To the extent this belief is true, vocational training needs to place greater emphasis on integrated learning, critical-thinking skills, and connections between vocational and academic skills, rather than on the mastery of the narrow, occupation-specific skills that characterized vocational education in the past. This new vision may also require broader changes in vocational education, including rethinking the organization, goals, content, and delivery of services, as well as the manner in which students and programs are assessed.

The educational measurement community is engaged in an equally serious rethinking of the structure of assessment (Wolf, 1992; Mehrens, 1992; Wiggins, 1989). Traditional, selected-response methods (multiple choice, matching, true-false) are being criticized for a variety of reasons: they can lead to narrowing of curriculum, test preparation practices may inflate scores in high-stakes situations, there are consistent differences in average performance between racial/ethnic and gender groups, etc. (Koretz, Linn, Dunbar, and Shepard, 1991; Shepard and Dougherty, 1991; Koretz et al., 1993; Shepard, 1991; Smith and Rothenberg, 1991). Many educators advocate the use of alternative approaches, including open-response items, realistic simulations, extended performance events, exhibitions, judged competitions, portfolios, and other forms of elaborated student demonstration.

Educators and researchers are working to find ways to improve the technical quality and feasibility of such performance-based assessments. With regard to the quality dimension, researchers are concerned about the consistency of scoring and of student performance; the fairness of assessments that demand complex, contextually rich responses; and the interpretability of scores. From a practical point of view, educators worry about the complexity and cost of developing and scoring performance assessments, the additional time burdens they impose on students and teachers, and their acceptability to key stakeholders, including the business community. On the positive side, the distinguishing feature of most alternative assessments is "authenticity," i.e., students perform an activity or task as it would be done in practice rather than selecting from a fixed set of alternatives. On their face, these activities have greater validity than selected-response tests because success is clearly related to the criterion of interest, be it writing, problem solving, or performing job tasks. On the negative side, a student's performance on complex tasks is not as consistent from one task to the next as it is with selected-response items, and the scores produced by alternative assessments are not as dependable or interpretable as those produced by traditional tests (Shavelson, Baxter, and Pine, 1992; Shavelson, Gao, and Baxter, 1993; Koretz, Stecher, Klein, and McCaffrey, 1994). These issues are unresolved at present, and there appear to be trade-offs among quality and feasibility considerations.

The uncertainties surrounding vocational education and educational assessment provide the context for our inquiry into vocational education assessment. Many educators believe that assessment can play an important role in systemic educational changes such as those being envisioned for vocational education (Wolf, 1992). The question we are exploring is: What forms of assessment might best meet the needs of vocational education, and how can educators make intelligent choices among the alternatives? Our evaluation of the alternatives paid particular attention to the purposes for which the assessment was to be used, the quality of the information provided, and the practicality or feasibility of the assessment approach.

PURPOSE AND PROCEDURES

Our project, which ran from 1994 to 1996, had a twofold purpose: (1) to provide information about promising alternative assessments that may meet the needs of vocational educators, and (2) to develop materials to help vocational educators make better decisions regarding the use of alternative assessments. This report addresses the first goal, i.e., it evaluates alternative assessments in the context of the current needs of vocational educators. To that end, we gathered information about selected assessment systems, summarized it in a set of detailed case descriptions, reviewed it critically from the perspective of vocational education, and identified some of the important factors that affect the choice of assessments in the vocational context. The second goal was to convert our knowledge into training and evaluation materials useful to vocational educators and to other groups considering assessment reforms in similar contexts. These are to be published as a practitioner guide by the National Center for Research in Vocational Education in 1997.

We began our investigation broadly, reviewing the literature and contacting experts in the field to look for promising examples of operational assessment systems applicable to vocational education. We developed a set of frameworks for organizing our thinking about the needs of vocational educators and for classifying types of assessment, uses of assessment, and dimensions of assessment quality. These ideas are reflected in our discussions about the needs of vocational educators in Chapter Two and the range of alternative assessments in Chapter Three. We then identified a tentative list of exemplary alternative assessments—both within vocational education and in related education and training sectors. For each project, we collected initial descriptive data from the printed record and from telephone interviews. We then compiled these data into a working casebook.

A panel of expert advisors familiar with vocational education and assessment was formed to guide our work from both technical and practitioner perspectives and to select the assessment reform efforts that would be reviewed in depth. The panel met in March of 1995 and offered advice about our selection of cases and plans for organizing information. To achieve our goal of providing vocational educators with relevant information and helpful procedures for selecting (or developing) alternative assessments, the panel members felt it was important to include a diverse set of assessments in our sample. They encouraged us to select assessment cases that differed in terms of their purposes and the uses of the results, the types of knowledge and skills being assessed, the types of assessment strategies being used, and the organization and structure of the assessment system.

With these factors in mind, we selected six cases for in-depth investigation:

- Career-Technical Assessment Program (C-TAP)

- Kentucky Instructional Results Information System (KIRIS)

- Laborers-AGC (Associated General Contractors) environmental training and certification programs

- National Board for Professional Teaching Standards (NBPTS) certification program

- Oklahoma Department of Vocational-Technical Education competency-based testing program

- Vocational/Industrial Clubs of America (VICA) national competition

We developed a common set of questions to guide our examination of the six cases. The questions focused on description, implementation, administration, consequences, feasibility, quality, and applicability to vocational education. We gathered information to address these questions from a variety of sources, including descriptive materials provided by the assessment activities, the research literature, telephone interviews, and one- to two-day site visits. During the site visits (which involved four of the six cases), we interviewed staff and observed various activities.

After the data were collected, we constructed a thorough description of each assessment, including the features we deemed to be most relevant to vocational education. Each member of the research team assumed primary responsibility for one of the assessment activities. This person coordinated the data collection and was responsible for writing up the case summary according to a common format. One person assumed an editorial role and rewrote the case summaries to provide greater consistency of presentation and voice. We were not formally evaluating each of the efforts and did not attempt to reach a conclusive judgment about each one. When questions could not be answered via available sources, we left them unresolved; when there was disagreement among sources or other contradictory information, we reported the differences. Finally, we conducted an impressionistic review of the case reports, looking for insights that would be relevant to vocational educators.

The next section briefly describes the cases studied. Subsequent chapters use these cases to illustrate the range of concerns and choices that confront vocational educators. Specifically, Chapter Two discusses the educational uses of assessment and the specific needs of vocational educators, Chapter Three describes various types of measures that vocational educators might use, and Chapter Four presents the factors that might affect the choice of assessment, including the quality of the information provided and the feasibility of various options. In each instance, we present information from the cases to illustrate the issues being discussed.

Our sample was both too small and too diverse to permit strong generalizations about the type of assessment to use in a particular situation. Instead, it provided illustrations of a variety of trade-offs that confront the developers of educational assessments, trade-offs that are relevant to vocational educators as well. In Chapter Five, we discuss these trade-offs, presenting illustrations drawn from the cases and relating these cases to the vocational education context. In the concluding chapter, we consider two prominent assessment challenges facing vocational educators—improving programs and certifying occupational mastery—and draw some implications from our study for selecting or developing assessments to support those functions.

A note on terminology: The collection of assessment activities we reviewed was quite diverse, creating minor problems in description. The sample ranges from developmental efforts (C-TAP) to fully operational testing programs (Laborers-AGC); from job-specific measures (VICA) to broader, occupational assessments (NBPTS); and from single tests (Oklahoma) to assessment systems (KIRIS). Because of this diversity, it is difficult to find simple terminology to refer to all these assessment efforts. They are not all "tests" in the traditional use of the word, nor are they all "testing programs." We use the terms *assessment, assessment activity,* and *accountability system* to refer to our cases in general. When discussing a specific case, we often use a narrower, more focused term, such as *test* or *measure,* as appropriate.

BRIEF DESCRIPTION OF CASES

This section briefly summarizes the six assessment activities to familiarize the reader with the range of our sample and the variety of approaches represented. More thorough descriptions of the six assessment activities are contained in Appendices A through F.

Career-Technical Assessment Program

The Career-Technical Assessment Program (C-TAP) is a standards-based assessment system designed to support instruction of important career skills and assess the preparedness of California students for entry-level jobs and postsecondary educational training. The program was developed by WestEd under the direction of the California Department of Education (CDE) and the Sacramento County Office of Education (SCOE). C-TAP assessments are being implemented in five career areas: agriculture, business, health careers, home economics, and industrial and technology education. Originally, in 1990, C-TAP was planned as a set of specific occupational tests for over twenty-nine occupations, and C-TAP's primary purpose was to be a standardized statewide student certification system. However, C-TAP's purpose and content have changed over time. The focus switched from specific occupations and job skills to clusters of related occupations and broader skills, and expanded to include cumulative assessment components. The C-TAP assessment system includes three components, each of which addresses academic skills, general workplace skills, and job-specific skills: (1) the portfolio, (2) the project, and (3) the written scenario. Scoring for the portfolios, projects, and written scenarios is done by teachers, using scoring rubrics designed by WestEd. C-TAP was recently expanded to include *multiple choice and short written-response questions.* These on-demand components are designed to measure the breadth of students' career-technical knowledge. They will be administered and scored by CDE. C-TAP is currently being used primarily as a teaching/learning tool and as an assessment contributing to grades in vocational education programs. It is not yet widely used in any standardized fashion; rather, teachers tend to adapt the materials for use in their own classrooms. The portfolio is generally deemed to be the strongest component of C-TAP by teachers using the system. Widespread adoption of portfolios by individual teachers appears to be feasible, if teachers can find time to learn how to use them and agree that substantive course material may have to be dropped, at least initially, to free up time for their use.

Kentucky Instructional Results Information System

The Kentucky Instructional Results Information System (KIRIS) is a statewide assessment system for elementary and secondary schools that is part of a major reform of public education in Kentucky. Designed both as an accountability tool and as a lever to promote changes in curriculum and instruction, KIRIS uses multiple measures of achievement, including open-ended written questions, group performance events, and portfolios of students' best work to produce school-level scores. Also factored into a school's accountability score are two noncognitive measures, attendance and retention. Significant rewards are attached to success (schools can earn thousands of dollars for high performance) and significant penalties to failure (the threat of external intervention for continued failure to improve performance). Partially as a result, KIRIS has affected teacher behavior and brought about changes in schools that are consistent with the larger state reform effort. But stakeholders have raised questions about the quality of the scores and the fairness of the awards. Independent evaluations have identified technical shortcomings that threaten the validity of the awards and of school comparisons (Hambleton et al., 1995). Kentucky educators are working to respond to these concerns and to improve the system.

Laborers-AGC Environmental Training and Certification Programs

The Laborers International Union of North America and the Associated General Contractors of America (AGC) cooperatively fund and manage a program of courses and assessments whose purpose is to train and certify environmental cleanup workers (and construction laborers). The courses, which are taught at affiliated local training schools, must comply with federal government regulations that focus on avoiding potential threats to health and safety. The assessment system includes both performance events with real equipment (which take place multiple times during the course) and criterion-referenced multiple-choice tests (which occur at the end). The assessments are used to certify each individual's competence, as well as to monitor program success and report program completion information. In the last few years, Laborers-AGC has started to evaluate and strengthen the technical quality of its environmental assess-

used to compare and reward programs, accountability assessments also should demonstrate a high degree of reliability and validity.

Our case studies demonstrate the full range of purposes, as shown in Table 1.

VOCATIONAL PROGRAM CONTEXT

Vocational educators need assessments that are sensitive to the unique features of the vocational context. In particular, vocational educators face changes in the nature of the students enrolling in vocational courses and in the nature of skills being taught in those courses. Both features need to be understood to make wise assessment choices.

Vocational Student Population

The educational objectives and course-taking behaviors of vocational students at the secondary level differ from those of vocational

Table 1

Purposes of Assessments in the Sample

Assessment Activity	Measuring Individual Learning for Instructional Improvement	Certifying Mastery	Holding Programs Accountable
Career-Technical Assessment Program (C-TAP)	✔		
Kentucky Instructional Results Information System (KIRIS)	✔		✔
Laborers-AGC environmental training and certification programs	✔	✔	✔
National Board for Professional Teaching Standards (NBPTS) certification program		✔	
Oklahoma competency-based testing program	✔		✔
Vocational/Industrial Clubs of America (VICA) national competition	✔	✔	

students at the postsecondary level. As a result, secondary and postsecondary vocational programs may have different priorities for assessment.

At the secondary level, there has been a decrease in vocational course-taking in favor of more academic coursework. One consequence of this change may be that secondary vocational educators look to assessment as a course improvement tool more than they have in the past. Compared with the situation in the 1980s, students are taking fewer vocational courses, there are fewer vocational teachers, and there are fewer university programs training these teachers (Boesel and McFarland, 1994). Between 1982 and 1992 academic course-taking was up by 22 percent and vocational course-taking was down by 17 percent (Vocational Education Journal, 1995). Even with this trend, in 1992 almost all public high school graduates (97 percent) completed at least one vocational education course (Levesque et al., 1995, p. 7). Twenty-four percent of high school students were considered vocational concentrators, completing at least three credits in a single vocational program area.

Although secondary vocational education is often associated with students planning to go to work after high school, most seniors plan to go on to some form of postsecondary education—49 percent plan to attend a four-year college or university and 22 percent plan to attend a two-year college or technical, vocational, or trade school. Only 15 percent of seniors plan to work full time (MPR Associates, 1996). Rather than taking coordinated sequences of courses in an occupational area, vocational students take single vocational courses to learn more about a career or to learn a specific skill related to work (i.e., word processing). Consequently, the emphasis in secondary vocational programs is more on assessments that are relevant to students taking only one or two courses—i.e., more on those that provide information to improve learning and instruction than on those for certifying mastery of employment skills.

The enrollment pattern of vocational students at the postsecondary level is quite different, and the assessment needs of postsecondary vocational educators are thus different as well. In the late 1980s, postsecondary vocational enrollment increased at the same pace as enrollment in general. Thirty-five percent of all undergraduate students were enrolled in postsecondary vocational education. In non-baccalaureate programs, about one-half of these students reported majoring in a vocational area (Boesel and McFarland, 1994). Students in vocational courses vary in age, work experience, and career aspiration. More important, postsecondary vocational students have varying motives for enrolling in vocational education courses. Some students enroll in a course to advance their career or begin retraining for a new career. This creates a need for assessments that provide information on how to improve learning and instruction, as is the case at the secondary level. Other students enroll in a sequence of courses in order to enter a particular career or to be certified for a particular job. In this case, vocational educators need to be able to certify that students have mastered relevant skills. In addition, accountability requirements apply to students who complete sequences of vocational courses, and staff must have assessment data to evaluate the success of these programs.

Knowledge and Skills

Vocational education was created to prepare students for specific jobs, but many argue that this focus on narrow training should change (Lazerson and Grubb, 1974). In the early 1900s, there was strong support from the business community for the federal government to fund vocational education in order to alleviate the scarcity of "skilled" workers through "skill" education. Businessmen alleged that the rise of factories had made the existing apprenticeship system obsolete and that it was difficult and economically inefficient to rely on informal, on-the-job learning in modern factories (Lazerson and Grubb, 1974). Hence, in 1917 the Smith-Hughes Act granted federal funds to public schools to develop skill-oriented vocational education programs.

Since 1917, the U.S. economy and workplace have broadened and diversified, as have the goals for vocational education. The statement of purpose of the most current federal law, the 1990 Carl D. Perkins Vocational and Applied Technology Education Act (American Vocational Association, 1992), reads:

> It is the purpose of this Act to make the United States more competitive in the world economy by developing more fully the academic and occupational skills of all segments of the population. This purpose will principally be achieved through concentrating

resources on improving educational programs leading to academic and occupational skill competencies needed to work in a technologically advanced society.

Attitudes toward the teaching and learning of vocational skills have changed in two important ways. The first change has to do with the degree of specificity of work. Americans have learned to place greater value on broad skills that relate to a family or cluster of jobs than on narrow skills defined in terms of a single job. The second change relates to the "situatedness" of work. The understanding that skills do not exist in isolation but are defined by the way work is organized is taking hold. These two new points of view have implications for instruction and assessment in vocational education.

The first change concerns the specificity of job skills. Skills can be thought of as lying on a continuum between general workforce preparation and specific occupational skills. Table 2 provides an example of skills from the health occupations at four points on this continuum. At the most general level, workforce preparation consists of basic communication and computation, which may be offered within traditional academic disciplines or in broadly focused vocational courses. The second level comprises narrower, industry-

Table 2

Continuum of Knowledge and Skills: Examples from the Health Industry

General Workforce Preparation	Industry Core Skills and Knowledge	Occupational Cluster Skills	Specific Occupational Skills
All Workers	Health Services	Health Information Services	Health Information Technology
Read, write, perform mathematical operations, listen, and speak	Be aware of the history of health Use health care terminology	Locate information in medical records Use computer programs to process client information	Evaluate medical records for completeness and accuracy Use a computer program to assign patients to a diagnosis-related grouping

Chapter Three

TYPES OF ASSESSMENT

Interest in alternative types of assessment has grown rapidly during the 1990s, both as a response to dissatisfaction with multiple-choice and other selected-response tests and as an element in a systemic strategy to improve student outcomes. Alternative assessments range from written essays to hands-on performance tasks to cumulative portfolios of diverse work products. This chapter describes four types of alternative assessment that might meet the needs of vocational educators and summarizes assessments in use in the cases selected for our study. The chapter concludes with a brief discussion of the advantages and disadvantages of different types of assessment.

ALTERNATIVES TO SELECTED-RESPONSE ASSESSMENT

The most familiar form of assessment is one in which the test-taker is asked to select each response from a set of specified alternatives. Because the test-taker chooses an option rather than creating an answer from scratch, such an assessment is called a *selected-response* assessment. Such assessments include multiple-choice, matching, and true-false tests.

Alternatively, an assessment can require a student to develop his or her own answer in response to a stimulus, or prompt. An assessment of this form, such as one that requires an essay or a solution to a mathematical problem, is called a *constructed-response* assessment. Neither the prompts nor the responses need be written, however. Responses commonly include any form whose quality can be judged accurately, from live performances to accumulated work products.

For this reason, constructed-response assessments are also called *performance assessments.* In our study, we also used the less technical term *alternative assessment* as a synonym for both of these terms.

A major distinguishing feature of all constructed-response assessments is that humans must score the responses.[1] Someone must review each answer (be it an essay, performance, project, or portfolio), compare it to a standard, and decide whether it is acceptable. Human scoring is slower and more expensive than machine scoring. Furthermore, as the answers grow more complex, the scoring judgments are more difficult and subject to greater error.

There are a variety of ways to classify assessments (Hill and Larson, 1992; Herman, Aschbacher, and Winters, 1992). In fact, since the range of constructed-response types and situations is limitless and more formats are being developed all the time, it is unlikely that there will be a single best system of classification. For our purposes, we used categories developed by the National Center for Research in Vocational Education (NCRVE) that are clearly relevant to vocational educators (Rahn et al., 1995). There are four major categories of assessment strategies: written assessments, performance tasks, senior projects, and portfolios. As Table 4 shows, the written assessment category includes both selected- and constructed-response assessments, whereas the other three categories involve only constructed-response assessments.

The classification system is based primarily on format—how the questions are presented and how responses are produced. However, selected-response and constructed-response assessments differ in many other ways, including the complexity of their development, administration, and scoring; the time demands they place on students and teachers; their cost; and the cognitive demands they make on students. These differences are explored in the remainder of this chapter and Chapter Four.

---

[1]There have been recent advances in computerized scoring of constructed-response assessments, but these systems are still in the research phase and will not be widely available for years.

to write an essay evaluating a real-life situation and proposing a solution (such as determining why a calf is sick and proposing a cure).

Performance Tasks

Performance tasks are hands-on activities that require students to demonstrate their ability to perform certain actions. This category of assessment covers an extremely wide range of behaviors, including designing products or experiments, gathering information, tabulating and analyzing data, interpreting results, and preparing reports or presentations. In the vocational context, performance tasks might include diagnosing a patient's condition based on a case study, planning and preparing a nutritionally balanced meal for a vegetarian, or identifying computer problems in an office and fixing them. Performance tasks are particularly attractive to vocational educators because they can be used to simulate real occupational settings and demands. Our cases included many examples of performance tasks. For instance, each Oklahoma vocational student had to complete two tasks designed and scored by his or her teachers. The VICA competitions primarily involved lifelike simulations, such as an emergency team responding to an accident victim.

The skills that must be demonstrated in performance tasks can vary considerably. Some tasks may demand that a student demonstrate his or her abilities in a straightforward way, much as was practiced in class (e.g., adjusting the spark plug gap). One health trainee assessment involved changing hospital bed sheets while the bed was occupied, a skill that participants had practiced frequently. Other tasks may present situations demanding that a student determine how to apply his or her learning in an unfamiliar context (e.g., figuring out what is causing an engine to run roughly). Teachers participating in the NBPTS certification process must respond to unanticipated instructional challenges presented during a day-long series of assessment exercises.

As assessments become more open ended and student responses become more complex, scoring grows more difficult. A variety of methods have been developed to score complex student performances, including both holistic and analytic approaches. In some cases, students are assessed directly on their performance; in other cases, assessment is based on a final product or oral presentation. For example, in the VICA culinary arts contest, students prepare platters of cold food and a multicourse meal of cooked food using the ingredients and equipment provided. Judges assess both the procedures used (by rating organizational skills, sanitation, and safety) and the final product (by rating presentation and taste). Similarly, in the KIRIS interdisciplinary performance events, students work together in groups on open-ended activities and then produce individual products. The group work is not judged, just the individual responses.

Traditionally, vocational educators have relied on performance-based assessment strategies to judge student mastery of job-specific skills. For example, an automotives teacher judges whether a student can change the oil of a car by asking him or her to perform the task. However, other strategies may be required if that teacher wants to assess a student's ability to understand the technical principles underlying an automotive engine.

Recently, researchers have developed performance tasks that can be administered and scored by computer. Such computer-based performance assessment systems are in the experimental stage, but the results of recent research are promising. Vocational educators may be able to add computer-based tools to their list of assessment alternatives in the not too distant future.

Two types of computerized assessment tools deserve attention. First, computers are being used to simulate interactive, real-world problems. For example, O'Neil, Allred, and Dennis (1992) developed a simulation of negotiation skills in which students interact with a computer as if they were negotiating with another individual. The researchers found strong evidence that the simulation provided a valid measure of interpersonal negotiation skills within the workplace context. It is easy to imagine other occupational skills that might be assessed using computer simulations. Second, expert computer systems are being developed that can review and score constructed responses. For example, Bennett and Sebrechts (1996) developed a computer system that scored student responses to algebra word problems. This system was as accurate as human judges in determining the correctness or incorrectness of student responses, although it was less effective in classifying student errors. Similar prototype systems have been used to score answers to programming problems, to analyze architectural design problems, and to identify student misconceptions in subtraction (Bennett and Sebrechts, 1996).

Although these results are encouraging, it will take considerable time before computer-based assessment tools are widely available. None of the cases we studied used computer-based assessments, and, with the exception of this brief look at the topic, we did not include them in our analyses. If this study were reconducted five years from now, we would expect much more attention to be given to these alternatives.

Senior Projects

Senior projects are distinct from written assessments and performance tasks because they are cumulative, i.e., they reflect work done over an extended period rather than in response to a particular prompt. The term *senior project* is used here to identify a particular type of culminating event in which students draw upon the skills they have developed over time. It has three components: a research paper, a product or activity, and an oral presentation, all associated with a single career-related theme or topic. The format is designed to be motivating, to permit involvement of people from business or community, and to encourage integration of academic and vocational ideas. For this reason, the process of implementing senior projects in a school often involves collaboration between teachers in many subjects who agree to guide the student's selection and accept the work for credit in more than one course.

All three components of a senior project are organized around a single subject or theme, such as a traditional method of making furniture, the creation of an appealing store window display, or a fashion show. To complete the research paper, the student must conduct research about aspects of the subject he or she has not previously studied. The student draws upon library and other resources and produces a formal written paper. The student then creates a product or conducts an activity relevant to the subject. This might include making something or doing community volunteer work for an extended period and documenting it. The purpose is to demonstrate knowledge or skills relevant to the subject. Finally, the student presents his or her work orally to a committee or at a public forum.

The length and complexity of the senior project make evaluation difficult. Schools that have implemented this type of assessment have spent a fair amount of time deciding how to judge the quality of the various elements. Their scoring guides reflect concerns about content, technical knowledge, organization and time management, the extension of knowledge outside traditional school domains, communication skills, and even appearance (Rahn et al., 1995, p. U3-12). These all involve subjective judgments, so great care must be taken to ensure that scores are accurate and meaningful.

Portfolios

Like a senior project, a portfolio is a cumulative assessment that represents a student's work and documents his or her performance. However, whereas a senior project focuses on a single theme, a portfolio may contain any of the forms of assessments described above plus additional materials such as work samples, official records, and student-written information. For example, in the C-TAP portfolio, students not only provide an artifact (or evidence of one if it is not portable) but give a class presentation that is evaluated as part of their project. Records may include transcripts, certificates, grades, recommendations, resumes, and journals. Portfolios also often contain a letter of introduction to the reader from the student explaining why each piece has been included. They may contain career development materials, letters from supervisors or employers, completed job applications, test results, and samples of work products. The contents may reflect academic accomplishment, industrial or career-related accomplishments, and personal skills.

Some portfolios are designed to represent the student's best work, others are designed to show how the student's work has evolved over time, and still others are comprehensive repositories for all the student's work. Both the KIRIS portfolios (for writing and mathematics) and the C-TAP portfolios (for a vocational area) are built around a selection of the student's best work. The C-TAP portfolio adds other types of assessment such as records (a resume) and a work artifact (a writing sample).

Portfolios present major scoring problems because each student includes different pieces. This variation makes it difficult to develop scoring criteria that can be applied consistently from one piece to the next and from one portfolio to the next. States that have begun to use portfolios on a large scale have had difficulty achieving acceptable quality in their scoring (Stecher and Herman, 1997), but they are making progress in this direction. One approach is to set guidelines for the contents of the portfolios so that they all contain similar components. Specific learner outcomes can be identified for each component and then techniques can be developed for assessing student performance in terms of these outcomes.

Table 5 shows the range of assessment types being used in the sites selected for this study.

COMPARING SELECTED-RESPONSE AND ALTERNATIVE ASSESSMENTS

For decades, selected-response tests (multiple-choice, matching, and true-false) have been the preferred technique for measuring student achievement, particularly in large-scale testing programs. In one form or another, selected-response measures have been used on a large scale for seventy-five years. Psychometricians have developed an extensive theory of multiple-choice testing, and test developers have accumulated a wealth of practical expertise with this form of assessment.

Nevertheless, there are limitations to using multiple-choice and other selected-response measures. First, these traditional forms of assessment may not measure certain kinds of knowledge and skills effectively. For example, it is difficult to measure writing ability with a multiple-choice test. Similarly, a teacher using cooperative learning arrangements in a classroom may find that selected-response measures cannot address many of the learning outcomes that are part of the unit, including teamwork, strategic planning, and oral communication skills. In these cases, multiple-choice tests can only provide indirect measures of the desired skills or abilities (e.g., knowledge of subject-verb agreement, capitalization, and punctuation, and the ability to recognize errors in text may serve as surrogates for a direct writing task). Users of the test results must make an inference from the score to the desired domain of performance.

Table 5

Types of Assessments in the Sample

| Assessment System | Selected Response | Constructed Response | | | | |
| | Written | | | | | |
	Multiple Choice	Open Ended	Essay, etc.	Performance	Senior Project	Portfolio
Career-Technical Assessment Program (C-TAP)			✓	✓		✓
Kentucky Instructional Results Information System (KIRIS)			✓	✓		✓
Laborers-AGC environmental training and certification programs	✓			✓		
National Board for Professional Teaching Standards (NBPTS) certification program			✓	✓		✓
Oklahoma competency-based testing program	✓			✓		
Vocational /Industrial Clubs of America (VICA) national competition	✓			✓		

Second, when used in high-stakes assessment programs, multiple-choice tests can have adverse effects on curriculum and instruction. Many standardized multiple-choice tests are designed to provide information about specific academic skills and knowledge. When teachers focus on raising test scores, they may emphasize drill, practice, and memorization without regard to the students' ability to transfer or integrate this knowledge. Instruction may focus on narrow content and skills instead of broader areas, such as critical thinking and problem solving (Miller and Legg, 1993). In addition, many think multiple-choice tests emphasize the wrong behaviors given that few people are faced with multiple-choice situations in their home or work lives (Wiggins, 1989).

During the past few years, constructed-response assessment approaches have gained popularity as tools for classroom assessment and large-scale use. Proponents of alternative forms of assessment believe they will alleviate some of the problems presented by multiple-choice tests. It is easier to measure a broader range of skills and ability using constructed-response approaches than selected-response approaches. To measure writing ability, one asks students to write; to test oral communication, one has students give oral reports. In addition, alternative assessments permit the use of complex, realistic problems instead of the narrow or decontextualized problems that appear on many multiple-choice tests. Because of this, teaching to alternative assessments is desirable, because good test preparation will be good instruction.

However, alternative assessments are not without problems. In fact, they may have many of the same flaws cited for multiple-choice tests. Critics argue that poorly designed alternative assessments can also be very narrow, so that teaching to them may also be undesirable. For example, mathematics portfolios may overemphasize "writing about mathematics" at the expense of learning mathematical procedures. In addition, alternative assessments have practical problems, including high cost, administrative complexity, low technical quality, and questionable legal defensibility (Mehrens, 1992). These flaws are of greatest concern when assessments are used to certify individuals for work or to reward or sanction people or systems. (These issues are discussed in greater detail in Chapters Four and Five.) Table 6 compares selected-response and constructed-response measures in terms of a number of important features.

Table 6

Features of Selected- and Constructed-Response Measures

Feature	Selected Response			Constructed Response		
	Rarely	Some-times	Usually	Rarely	Some-times	Usually
Easy to develop			✓	✓		
Easy to administer			✓		✓	
Easy to score			✓	✓		
Similar to real world in performance demands ("authentic")	✓					✓
Efficient (requires limited time)		✓		✓		
Credible to stakeholders			✓		✓	
Embodies desired learning activities	✓					✓
Sound basis for determining quality of scores			✓		✓	
Effective for factual knowledge			✓			✓
Effective for complex cognitive skills (e.g., problem solving)		✓				✓

Chapter Four

CRITERIA FOR COMPARING ASSESSMENTS: QUALITY AND FEASIBILITY

As the preceding chapter suggests, vocational educators are likely to find more than one assessment strategy that will serve their purpose. Two important criteria for deciding which assessment to use in a particular situation are the quality of the information provided and the feasibility of the assessment process. This chapter describes these criteria and compares selected- and constructed-response alternatives in terms of quality and feasibility.

Unfortunately, it is usually not possible to maximize both quality and feasibility, so vocational educators must strike a balance between them. As assessment becomes more authentic, it also becomes more expensive to develop, to administer, and to score. In addition, greater quality usually involves greater cost and greater commitment of time. There is no simple formula for balancing these factors. Ideally, educators would establish standards for quality based on the uses to which the information was to be put, and then allocate resources appropriate for meeting those standards. In addition, they would only impose practical constraints that did not limit quality. In reality, this balancing act is more an art than a science, but we believe an understanding of the factors will lead to better decisions.

QUALITY OF ASSESSMENTS

The relative quality of the available alternatives should be a factor in selecting an assessment strategy. Concerns about quality are particularly important when assessments are used to make critical decisions, such as certifying individual skill mastery or rewarding successful training programs. Vocational educators face such decisions regularly, so it is important that they understand something about the technical quality of assessments.

The quality of an assessment can be judged in terms of three questions:

- How accurate is the information?

- How confident can one be in the conclusions drawn about students or programs?

- Is the assessment fair to all students who take it?

These questions respectively correspond to the psychometric concepts of reliability, validity, and fairness. Given the present state of the art in alternative assessment, all approaches do not provide equally accurate information, support desired interpretations equally well, or provide all students with equivalent and fair challenges. Table 7 summarizes some of the quality differences between selected- and constructed-response measures, which are elaborated below.

Table 7

Quality of Information of Selected- and Constructed-Response Measures

Dimension of Quality	Selected Response	Constructed Response
Reliability	Automatic scoring is essentially error free	Rating process can increase error
	Many responses per topic increases consistency of score	Fewer responses per topic reduces consistency of score
	Strong theoretical basis for measuring reliability	Greater between-task variability in student performance
Validity	Large inferences from item to occupational behavior	Greater match between assessment task and real-world demands
		Variation in administration conditions can complicate interpretation of results
Fairness	Quantitative techniques help identify potential unfairness	May have greater fairness because tasks are more authentic

Reliability

There are no perfect measuring tools in science, in the kitchen, or in education, so people who use tools to measure things need to know how much error there is likely to be in the information they receive. Reliability is a numerical index of the degree to which an individual measurement (such as blood pressure, volume of liquid, or a test score) is free from error. There are a number of ways to determine whether a household or scientific measurement is accurate: repeat it with the same tool or a comparable tool, have someone else make the measurement, etc. Similar techniques are used to assess the reliability of educational measurements. Researchers try to answer the following questions:

- If the assessment were given again, would the same results be produced (test-retest reliability)?

- If students responded to a highly similar assessment, would the same results be produced (parallel-forms reliability)?

- If student responses were read by a different group of experts, would the same scores be assigned (rater reliability)?

Each of these three factors may contribute error to the student's score. Moreover, the errors are additive, i.e., the overall reliability of the assessment is reduced by each one. A reliable assessment is one in which scores are consistent across time, specific questions, readers, and other circumstances.

Reliability can be estimated mathematically on a scale from zero to one, with one representing the highest possible reliability. One form of selected-response assessment, commercial multiple-choice tests, usually produces score reliabilities of 0.80 and above using methods such as test-retest or parallel forms. The acceptable standard may be higher (0.90 or more) when tests are used for important decisions. Commercial tests employ a number of techniques to achieve these high levels of accuracy—e.g., they use selected-response options that control the range of possible answers, they have the results scored by machines, they use test development principles drawn from years of experience, and they include many questions about a given topic. This last technique increases the amount of information provided by the assessment in a given amount of time and reduces inconsistencies related to the specific questions asked. The Oklahoma assessments follow this model, and their reliability is quite high.

It is difficult to achieve equally high levels of reliability with constructed-response assessments. All of the sources of error mentioned above reduce the consistency of scores from performance assessments. For example, scoring introduces errors not present with selected-response measures. Rather than having an answer sheet being scored with almost perfect accuracy by a machine, human raters review essays, science projects, or pieces in a portfolio and assign scores on one or more dimensions. Both the C-TAP and Kentucky portfolios require expert readers to review the material and assign scores using a general rubric. The same is true for the NBPTS assessment activities. In all these cases, readers must make subjective judgments about the quality of complex student work, introducing inconsistencies that lower the accuracy of the scores.

There are methods to improve reader reliability. As educators become more familiar with alternative assessments, they are developing more accurate scoring procedures. For example, when scoring rubrics are aligned to specific tasks and carefully selected examples of student work are used as "anchors" for each score point, readers can score constructed-response questions with a high degree of consistency. Reports of high interreader consistency (above 0.80) are becoming more common. However, reader reliability is only one source of error in scores.

A second reason constructed-response assessments are less reliable than selected-response tests is that students do not perform as consistently on them. Research in a number of fields has found that a student's responses vary more from task to task on constructed-response measures than on selected-response measures. As the demands of the task increase (in terms of complexity, breadth, integratedness, or any number of factors), consistency of performance (and therefore reliability) declines. Thus, for example, there may be differences between two pieces of cabinetry produced by the same student, which means that his or her scores on joinery might differ depending on which piece is rated.

Furthermore, because constructed responses are more complex and time-consuming than selected responses, less information can be gathered in a given amount of time. For example, Kentucky performance events take a full class period and produce only one or two pieces of information about each participant. Similarly, students receive only a handful of scores on the Kentucky portfolios, which reflect many hours of work. With fewer pieces of information and greater variation between pieces, the judgment of skill or ability will be less accurate.

One consequence of the variation in performance is that more tasks are needed to produce a reliable score (Linn, 1993). Shavelson, Gao, and Baxter (1993) analyzed three different performance assessments (in science and mathematics) and reported that students would need to complete eight tasks on one of them, fifteen on another, and twenty-three on the remaining one to produce scores with acceptable reliability. Baker (1992) found that students would have to complete six or more history tasks (in which students read primary source documents and write essays explaining the important issues) to produce a score with reliability greater than 0.70. These results, and similar ones summarized by Linn (1993), mean that alternative assessments require considerably more time than selected-response tests to produce equally reliable scores. This translates into more development time, more classroom time, and greater cost (a problem addressed later in this chapter, in the feasibility discussion).

Validity

Scores can be accurate in the sense of being reliable and yet be used to draw wrong inferences. This is a problem of validity. For example, a student who knows how to solve applied mathematical problems may perform poorly on a written test of word problems because of reading difficulties. The test score may be reliable (i.e., the student consistently makes mistakes on written word problems), but to say the score means that the student does not know how to solve word problems in general would be incorrect.

An inference from a score is said to be valid if it is justified. Whereas reliability is a feature of the measure, validity is a feature of the way scores are interpreted by users. Consequently, assessments that are valid for one purpose may not be valid for another. For example, one might give a person studying to be a medical records clerk a multiple-choice test of spelling, grammar, and syntax to determine his or her ability to identify errors in textual material. However, the same test might not provide a good measure of the student's ability to write grammatically correct information on a record.

One of the primary motivations for adopting alternative assessments is to increase the validity of the inferences by making the assessment tasks more like the real-world activities the tests are supposed to reflect (Linn, Baker, and Dunbar, 1992). Selected-response measures constrain the assessment to a rigid format, which can narrow the types of skills that are measured. Constructed-response assessments present students with tasks that are more "authentic," i.e., that match more closely the activities performed in practice. The hope is that the resulting scores will provide a better measure of the domain of interest than will those on a multiple-choice test. The Laborers-AGC environmental performance assessment duplicates conditions of the job, and success on this assessment is thought to be highly predictive of success on the job.

There are several approaches that can be used to help establish the validity of an assessment for a particular purpose:

- Experts can review the content of the assessment and confirm that it is measuring the desired skills or behaviors (*content validity*).

- Results can be compared with performance in a work setting, either at the same time or in the future (*concurrent validity* or *predictive validity*). If people who do well on the assessment outperform those who do poorly on it, greater confidence can be placed in the assessment's ability to indicate job preparation.

- Results can be compared with those from other high-quality assessments of similar and dissimilar skills (*construct validity*). If the pattern of responses makes sense (i.e., assessments of similar skills produce similar results while assessments of different skills do not), greater confidence can be placed in the new assessment's ability to measure the skills it is supposed to be measuring.

- Consequences from using the assessment can be examined to shed light on the meaning of the results (*consequential validity*).

The first approach, content validity, is quite commonly used as the initial step in building a case about the interpretation of assessment results. If the tasks to be performed are identical to tasks on the job, as they are in the case of Laborers-AGC, content validity may be adequate to satisfy the users of the information. The government is satisfied that mastery of the AGC performance tasks produces competent workers. Similarly, the standards that underlie the NBPTS assessments were developed by committees of experts who reached consensus on the critical features of accomplished teaching. Extensive professional review forms the basis for the NBPTS standards, the appropriateness of the specific tasks, and the passing scores.

The second approach, concurrent validity (same-time comparison) or predictive validity (future comparison), is based on the idea that a meaningful score will be positively related to real performance. For example, after vocational educators in Oklahoma determined that scores on multiple-choice tests were as good at predicting future job performance as scores on scenarios, which are lengthier, they deleted the scenarios from the assessment program. This saved time and expense without reducing the validity of the scores for their intended purpose.

The third approach, construct validity, may be the appropriate technique to use when the constructs being measured are complex and hard to define and when successful performance is a matter of judgment. Researchers evaluating KIRIS compared the trends in accountability scores with the trends in scores on the National Assessment of Educational Progress (NAEP) state assessment. They were looking for evidence that KIRIS scores reflect real changes in student achievement rather than unrelated factors such as test familiarization.

The fourth approach, consequential validity, examines the effects of the assessment on practice and uses this information in interpreting scores (Messick, 1989). For example, Shepard and Dougherty (1991) found that the use of multiple-choice tests in high-stakes situations led to an undesirable narrowing of the curriculum. Students began spending more time on isolated facts and procedures and less time on conceptual learning. The instructional domain was reduced, which affected the proper interpretation of the test scores. The potential for distortion of classroom activities is just as great for alternative assessment as for selected-response tests (Linn, Baker, and Dunbar, 1992). It is incumbent on the users of assessment results to investigate carefully the broader effects of the assessment system before interpreting the results.

Alternative assessments present an additional validity challenge because they often have unstandardized components. More traditional, selected-response assessments dictate both the form of the test and the procedures for administration. These controls are designed to ensure that everyone has the same opportunity to perform and no one has access to special assistance. Similar standardization is possible for some constructed-response measures, such as performance tasks, but other alternatives are inherently unstandardized. Variations in the content of the assessment or the conditions under which the assessment is administered make it more difficult to interpret the results. For example, senior projects and portfolios have built-in flexibility with respect to the conditions of performance and the content of the assessment. One student's C-TAP portfolio may contain different work artifacts and experiences than another's. Furthermore, students may not perform their work under the same conditions. In particular, teachers may offer different levels of support, making it hard to know how much of the work that went into the final product was actually the student's (Gearhart, Herman, Baker, and Whittaker, 1993). Even though it is possible to score individual portfolios using a common rubric, there may be questions about the meaning of the scores if they are based on different products done under different conditions.

Fairness

Users of assessments must take into account the fact that irrelevant factors, such as family background and experience, may affect the scores of certain students. Assessments are unfair, or biased, if students who are otherwise equal in the skill being measured perform differently on a particular question because of experience or knowledge not related to the underlying skill. It is not easy to detect possible bias. The most commonly used techniques involve careful review of measures by committees trained to be sensitive to factors that might affect particular groups of students. Expert reviews were used by NBPTS to ensure that its certification system was fair to teachers regardless of their population group or the socioeconomic status of their students. Complicated statistical procedures can be used to determine whether test items are biased, but the results of these procedures are often confusing. Researchers have often found it difficult to understand what features of items lead to the differences they detect.

Many advocates of alternative assessments believe that these techniques, compared to selected-response measures, are more equitable to all groups because they involve more complete tasks and permit students to address the tasks in ways that are meaningful to them. However, there has been very little rigorous research on the fairness of alternative assessments. At least one study found evidence of unfairness of an unanticipated sort: minority students made poorer selections of pieces to include in their writing portfolios than did nonminority students (LeMahieu, 1993). If vocational educators are going to assess students from diverse backgrounds, they need to be sensitive to potential unfairness in the measures they select.

FEASIBILITY OF ASSESSMENTS

Practical considerations also play an important role in deciding what form of assessment to use. Selected-response tests are a model of efficiency, whereas alternative assessments can be more difficult to develop, more time-consuming to administer, and more troublesome to score, and can yield results that are more difficult to explain. That is not to say that alternative assessments lack positive features, but potential users need to be concerned about feasibility issues such as cost, time commitments, complexity, and credibility to key stakeholders. These features are summarized in Table 8 and discussed below.

Cost

In general, alternative assessments are more expensive to develop, administer, and score than are selected-response tests. The U.S. Congress, Office of Technology Assessment (1992) estimates that performance assessments are three to ten times as expensive as

Table 8

Feasibility of Selected- and Constructed-Response Measures

Dimension of Feasibility	Selected Response	Constructed Response
Cost	Relatively inexpensive to develop, administer, and score	More expensive to develop, administer, and score Teachers benefit from participation in scoring
Time	Efficient use of class time Few demands on teacher preparation time	Additional class time consumed More teacher preparation time needed If embedded, may not consume class time
Complexity	Relatively easy for developers and users	May require special skills to develop May need special materials to administer Difficult judgments make scoring difficult
Credibility	Familiar and well known Higher reliability leads to greater confidence	Growing popularity among educators Unfamiliar to community members Credibility with employers

multiple-choice assessments on a per-student basis, and more recent evidence suggests that in some cases these estimates may be low (Stecher and Klein, in press). For example, the prorated cost of one class period of multiple-choice science assessment is less than $1 per student. California spent about twice this amount to conduct its 1993 statewide assessment in science, which involved about one class period of hands-on activity (Comfort, 1995). Doolittle (1995) reported total costs for the State Collaborative on Assessment and Student Standards (SCASS) science tests of $11 to $14 per student for a similar amount of testing time. Stecher and Klein (in press) found the cost of one period of hands-on science assessment involving equipment and materials to be over $30 per pupil.

A number of factors contribute to the added cost of performance assessments. The tasks themselves often are more complex than selected-response items, so they require more time to draft, pilot, and revise before final versions are ready. Performance assessments can also be more difficult to administer, particularly if they involve the use of equipment, the collection of work products over time, or repeated review and revision of student responses. The additional costs occur in most cases because teachers have to be trained to follow more complicated administrative procedures. Even portfolios, which would appear to entail very little in the way of added administrative requirements, are not without added burden. Teachers in Vermont reported spending three hours per month of class time just organizing and managing portfolios (Koretz, Stecher, Klein, and McCaffrey, 1994). Some assessments use external administrators, rather than teachers, as a way to guarantee comparability of administration, which also increases costs. (This is the model NAEP uses.)

In addition, student responses must be scored by hand rather than by machine, which is probably the most expensive part of the process. Scoring alternative assessments can be many times more expensive than scoring selected-response tests. For example, it costs pennies per student per class period to score multiple-choice tests and produce detailed score reports. By contrast, it costs dollars per class period per student to score essays, performance tasks, and portfolios and to produce one or two scores per student. Vermont teachers reported spending five hours per month of their own time scoring student portfolios during the year (Koretz et al., 1993). The Vermont Department of Education spent about $13 per student to score final student portfolios at the end of the year (Koretz, Stecher, Klein, and McCaffrey, 1994). Hardy (1995) reports scoring costs ranging from about $1.50 to $6 per student for performance assessments (depending on the length of the answer and whether it was scored once or twice). Commercial publishers charge about $5 per student for scoring writing assessments and reporting a single score, either holistic or analytic (Hoover and Bray, 1995). Stecher (1995) reports similar costs for scoring hands-on science assessments. In the cases we studied, the overall cost of NBPTS certification was extremely high, in part because of the complexity of judging candidate performance.

Although the amount of research on assessment cost is quite limited, there appears to be considerable variation in cost from one form of assessment to another. For example, it appears to be far easier to develop a writing prompt than a hands-on science task. Hoover and

Bray (1995) report the total cost of developing forty writing prompts for the Iowa Writing Assessment to be $138,000 (or about $3,500 per prompt), with an additional $175,000 (or $4,000 per prompt) for scoring during the field-test phase. Stecher and Klein (in press) report spending about $70,000 on average to develop one class period of hands-on science assessment. These differing development costs are due primarily to differences in the amount of time required; the cost of the science equipment was relatively small compared to the cost of the professional time. Similar differences in scoring costs among types of assessments are reported above.

Because of the wide variation in reported costs, it is not possible to develop handy rules of thumb for the time or cost of developing alternative assessments. It appears to be the case that costs increase as the assessment becomes less constrained (i.e., more "authentic") and more complex. Beyond that, there seems to be little agreement about how much time or money alternative assessments require. Computer-based assessments, discussed briefly in Chapter Two, may prove to be less expensive if they can be used on a large scale.

When thinking about differences in cost between alternative assessments and traditional, selected-response tests, it is important to consider differences in reliability as well. Most of the comparisons of assessment costs presented above are based on similar amounts of testing time, but not on equally reliable scores. For example, hands-on science tests were thirty times as expensive as multiple-choice science tests for one class period of assessment (Stecher and Klein, in press). However, three periods of hands-on science assessment were required to produce a student score as reliable as that from one period of multiple-choice testing. As a result, the cost ratio for equally reliable scores was ninety to one, rather than thirty to one.

Finally, it would be incorrect to consider costs without also mentioning benefits. The use of alternative assessments may have positive effects in the form of staff development that offset some of the costs. Teachers report that scoring performance assessments is an effective training activity. The process of reviewing student work and evaluating it against well-defined rubrics helps teachers develop a better appreciation for the range of student performance, weaknesses in student presentations, common misconceptions and problems encountered by students, the alignment between curriculum and assessment, and other features that relate to instructional planning. In this way, the scoring experience may improve teaching and learning. If this is the case, then it becomes important to know how valuable these benefits are. For example, would they be more efficiently achieved directly through targeted staff development than indirectly through assessment development and scoring activities? To date, such questions remain unexplored in the research on alternative assessment.

Time

In addition to costs that must be borne directly, alternative assessments place greater time demands on administrators, teachers, and students. For example, alternative assessments usually require more class time to administer than do selected-response tests. The use of class time for assessment can have negative consequences on instruction. Scoring also commands a great deal of time. There are advantages to having teachers score their own students' work. For example, they learn more about student performance, and there is no added cost for hiring outside scorers. However, scoring is an extremely time-consuming task, and teachers should be aware of the demands it may place on their preparation time.

When assessments are embedded in classroom instruction, such as is the case for senior projects and portfolios, the distinction between assessment time and learning time is blurred and the time problem is less troublesome. This is true of C-TAP and the KIRIS portfolios. These assessments do not place the significant additional demands on classroom time that stand-alone performance assessments do.

Complexity

Alternative assessments are more complex than traditional tests in a number of ways, including the situations that prompt student responses, the kinds of materials involved, the scope of the tasks, the cognitive demands placed on students, the procedures for collecting responses, and the procedures for scoring. As noted above, it is partly this complexity that makes alternative assessments more difficult to develop, administer, and score, which increases their cost. The complexity also demands more sophistication on the part of

users. For example, it can be more complicated to administer performance assessments that involve equipment and materials, than to
administer pencil-and-paper tests. In the case of Laborers-AGC, the
tasks can include the use of heavy machinery, hazardous materials,
and dangerous working conditions. The equipment makes administration more complex and places greater demands on task administrators, who need to be specially trained to work under these circumstances. Similarly, it may take greater expertise to, say, develop
good portfolio tasks or devise scoring rubrics for senior projects than
to administer and score selected-response tests. The additional
complexity inherent in alternative assessments may create practical
problems for some educators and some educational settings.
Additional training may be required, as well as additional equipment
and materials, storage space, and facilities for assessment.

Credibility

To have any practical value, alternative assessments, like all assessments, must provide information that is credible to the people who
use the results. In the case of vocational assessment, those who use
the results include not only the usual educational audiences
(students, teachers, and program directors), but potential employers,
labor leaders, and other community members as well. If an assessment fails to meet reasonable technical standards, its credibility may
decline in the eyes of some audiences. For example, Kentucky
teachers still have doubts about the appropriateness of KIRIS as an
accountability tool. Moreover, people who are familiar only with
traditional tests may not place much trust in scores generated by
such items as performance tasks, senior projects, or portfolios, even
if these forms of assessment are found to be reliable and valid. Part
of this discomfort may stem from unfamiliarity, a problem that
should be resolvable with training. On the other hand, one of the advantages of alternative assessments is that employers and other
stakeholders may give greater credibility to scores based on authentic performances than to scores from traditional tests. It appears that
this has been the case for the Laborers-AGC environmental program
and for the NBPTS certification program. It is true for VICA as well.

Chapter Five

OTHER ISSUES IN ASSESSMENT PLANNING

Quality and feasibility are important factors in assessment planning, but they do not always present themselves in the general ways discussed in Chapter Four. Our case studies produced examples of six other administrative considerations related to quality and feasibility that also play a significant role in assessment planning. Not all programs will need to address all of these issues, but as a set they illustrate the additional complexities that may arise. These six additional considerations are

1. Single versus multiple measures

2. High versus low stakes

3. Stand-alone versus embedded tasks

4. Standardization versus adaptability

5. Single versus multiple purposes

6. Voluntary versus mandatory participation

SINGLE VERSUS MULTIPLE MEASURES

There are obvious advantages to basing an assessment on a single measure, but there are reasons to prefer multiple measures as well. We saw both options in our case studies. Although the Oklahoma assessment program contains both performance assessments and standardized multiple-choice tests, Oklahoma relies on the multiple-choice test to determine whether individual students have mastered the curriculum in each vocational area. Each entrant in a particular

VICA competition completes just one occupational task. It might be argued that the C-TAP portfolio is also a single measure, but, in reality, it subsumes many measures. The C-TAP portfolios can contain other kinds of assessment results, such as test scores or competitive awards.

The principal advantage of single measures is efficiency (see Table 9). Oklahoma provides a good example of this. In the past, the Oklahoma state vocational testing program had two elements: multiple-choice items and realistic scenarios followed by sets of related questions. The scenarios were more complex to develop and score, and the Oklahoma Department of Education decided that the multiple-choice items did an adequate job of predicting job-related performance. As a result, the scenarios were dropped from the testing program, leading to a reduction in cost and resource demands. Similarly, VICA made a determination that a single performance event was adequate for a competition whose goals are primarily honorary. Even with this simplification, however, VICA finds it quite difficult to prepare the task specifications and scoring guides and to train the raters for a single activity per occupation. Multiple activities would be prohibitively time-consuming and expensive.

Educational researchers recommend the use of multiple measures primarily to provide the validity that comes from having alternative windows on behavior. NBPTS strongly believes in multiple measures, arguing that the job of teaching cannot be captured in a single type of assessment. Laborers-AGC uses both a multiple-choice test of knowledge and a performance test of a candidate's ability to carry out essential job tasks. Particularly where health and safety issues

Table 9

Advantages of Single Versus Multiple Measures

Single Measure	Multiple Measures
Efficiency of planning, administration, and scoring	Includes different types of skills and abilities
Reduced time and cost	Greater acceptability for evaluation of student performance (i.e., greater validity)
	Drives programs toward more comprehensive curriculum and instruction

are concerned, the government dictates that candidates must demonstrate both job-related knowledge and the ability to perform essential tasks. KIRIS combines three types of student achievement measures (open-ended individual tasks, group performance events and individual portfolios) and noncognitive measures (attendance, retention, etc.) into a single school accountability index. This approach is seen as providing a more complete picture of the multiple outcomes of schooling. The added quality comes at a price, however, because multiple measures are more time-consuming to develop, administer, and score.

A second advantage associated with multiple measures is that they foster the use of varied types of instruction and preparation. In high-stakes situations, single measures can lead to an undesirable narrowing of instructional content and strategies (Shepard and Dougherty, 1991; Koretz, Linn, Dunbar, and Shepard, 1991). Under the same conditions, it is better to send richer signals to teachers and to push them to prepare students to succeed in many assessment situations.

HIGH VERSUS LOW STAKES

Many aspects of an assessment are affected by the consequences attached to the use of its results. The stakes—i.e., the degree to which the outcome is associated with important rewards or penalties—can affect the character of the assessment, its credibility, the validity of scores, and the influence it has on instruction (see Table 10). Assessment may have high stakes for individuals, programs, or schools. For example, a person will be denied certain jobs in the en-

Table 10

Advantages of High Versus Low Stakes

High Stakes	Low Stakes
Greater motivation to perform well on the assessment	Less pressure to "teach to the test"
Greater emphasis on teaching the skills being assessed	More cooperative (rather than competitive) atmosphere
	Lower cost to develop and score
	Less critical need to ensure high reliability and validity

vironmental hazard industry if he or she fails to pass the relevant Laborers-AGC examination. NBPTS hopes that teachers who pass its certification assessment will earn respect, position, and eventually greater rewards because of their proven skills. KIRIS, in contrast, has no consequences for individual students but has serious consequences for schools. Continued high performance may lead to financial rewards for teachers, and continued low performance can lead to intervention by the Kentucky Department of Education.

High stakes have two major effects: they lead to greater scrutiny of results, and they influence people's behaviors in anticipation of the assessment. A licensing examination serves as a good example of the first situation, and NBPTS comes closest to that model in the cases we studied. Certification carries with it valued consequences—in at least one state, NBPTS-certified teachers receive a salary bonus. Because the certification results in a valued outcome, teachers must have confidence in the process. There have been many instances in which both licensing and employment assessments have been challenged in court by people who failed to pass and therefore were denied a benefit. For this reason, technical quality is an essential element of high-stakes assessments. When stakes are low, as in the case of most classroom testing, tests are rarely subjected to such careful review.

A consequence of the premium on technical quality is that more time must be devoted to development and more research put into measuring reliability and validity. As a result, high-stakes assessments can be far more costly than low-stakes assessments. KIRIS models some of these conditions. Since rewards are based on improvements in school accountability scores, the Kentucky Department of Education must ensure the quality of the scores. This necessitates additional research and development with their associated costs.

The second effect of high stakes, changes in people's behavior, may also affect the meaning of assessment results. In the case of VICA, individual levels of interest and anxiety affect contestants' performance, so scores may not truly reflect performance under real-world conditions. Stakes may also drive teachers to unusual behaviors, both desired and undesired. In the case of KIRIS, researchers have detected both positive changes in curriculum emphasis and negative increases in inappropriate test preparation practices (Koretz, Mitchell, Barron, and Stecher, 1996).

Neither of these negative effects is found to any substantial degree when tests have low stakes. However, low-stakes tests have their own drawbacks. Test-takers may put less effort into their performance, leading to scores that do not represent their true abilities. And teachers may not be as motivated to make sure students learn the concepts being tested as they would be if the scores "counted" for something.

STAND-ALONE VERSUS EMBEDDED TASKS

Traditionally, tests are distinct events that follow, but are not part of, an ongoing learning process. Assessments stand alone, administered at the culmination of a set of learning activities. For example, when Laborers-AGC environmental trainees complete a safety unit, each must demonstrate mastery of that unit by passing a performance test. Similarly, the VICA skills competitions occur as a culminating activity after classroom training.

Stand-alone assessments have both logical and practical advantages (see Table 11). They serve as markers for accumulated knowledge and skills, and they allow the assessment developer to design tasks without worrying about the specific instructional activities employed by each teacher. Focusing on content specifications independent of classroom implementation simplifies the design and administration of assessments.

Table 11

Advantages of Stand-Alone Versus Embedded Assessments

Stand Alone	Curriculum Embedded
Greater flexibility in designing assessments	More efficient use of class time
Greater standardization across classrooms	Greater connection with classroom lessons
Greater simplicity of administration	

An alternative approach is to embed the assessment, either by building assessment events into instructional activities as part of the curriculum or by gleaning products from meaningful learning activities to use in the assessment. (We use the term *curriculum-embedded* assessment to refer to both situations.) C-TAP and the portfolio component of KIRIS are the best examples of embedded assessments in the group we studied. As C-TAP students complete work internships, they capture evidence of their experience and include it in their portfolios. Similarly, Kentucky students select their best classroom products in writing and mathematics to include in their portfolios.

Embedded assessments have advantages as well. First, they may be more efficient in that they do not require teachers to set aside valuable class time for testing. However, the time efficiencies associated with this approach can be difficult to achieve in practice. For example, Kentucky students spend considerable class time preparing their portfolios—reviewing their work, selecting pieces, compiling their portfolios, and writing a reflective introduction to the work. Second, embedded assessments lead to judgments based on student products from less artificial conditions. Assessments are produced under regular school conditions and may be more typical of student work. However, since the conditions of performance are different for every classroom, it may be difficult to interpret class or school comparisons.

STANDARDIZATION VERSUS ADAPTABILITY

Most state testing programs are examples of standardized assessment systems, i.e., assessment conditions are the same in every location. Individual sites have little flexibility to change what is assessed or how it is measured. For example, the Oklahoma Department of Education develops and maintains the vocational testing program, and each institution implements the tests according to standardized procedures. Similarly, the Laborers-AGC assessment is planned centrally and administered in the same fashion at every site. NBPTS, KIRIS, and VICA are also centralized systems, but local teachers and programs have a degree of influence on selected aspects of these assessments. Kentucky teachers select the assignments that generate student work for the portfolio component of the assessments, NBPTS applicants provide materials drawn from their teaching experience, and active local VICA chapters can contribute to the planning of the national competitions. The most familiar form of adaptable assessment is classroom testing. Teachers are responsible for designing their own tests, and they implement them to meet their own classroom needs. C-TAP is an example of an adaptable assessment. Teachers adapt the portfolio framework to reflect their local emphases.

The advantages of a standardized approach include consistency of implementation and comparability of scores (see Table 12). All teachers administer the assessment according to the same rules, so results can be compared from one site to another. For example, comparable tests are given in each Oklahoma vocational program, and students who pass the test in one school are demonstrating the same mastery of materials as those who pass the tests in another. Similarly, students take the same constructed-response tests and participate in the same performance events throughout the state of Kentucky. All VICA contestants perform the same job-related tasks, as do all candidates for Laborers-AGC certification. Standardization is particularly important when high stakes are attached to the assessment. The pressures to perform well that can lead individual teachers and students to engage in inappropriate test preparation or administration activities are lessened when procedures are clearly standardized.

As Table 12 shows, adaptability has advantages as well. Most notably, it permits assessment to be more responsive to local needs. For example, teachers can customize C-TAP portfolios to their

Table 12

Advantages of Standardization Versus Adaptability

Standardized	Adaptable
Greater consistency of implementation	Greater sense of ownership among teachers (and of motivation among students)
Greater comparability of results across sites	Increased relevancy to local curriculum and community
	Increased meaningfulness to individual students

course and to the employer base in the surrounding neighborhood. Students who use the C-TAP portfolios in a health program thus include work samples related to health; those in a transportation program assemble work samples related to transportation. Permitting individual teachers to tailor the assessment to their local needs has other positive effects. For example, teachers may endorse the assessment more, because it can be made more relevant to their programs. This is an important rationale for using portfolios in the Vermont assessment program (Koretz, Linn, Dunbar, and Shepard, 1991).

It is possible to combine standardized and adaptable components, as is done in KIRIS. The on-demand components—open-ended questions and performance events—are the same everywhere, while the portfolios differ from class to class based on the tasks assigned by the local teachers. Similarly, the NBPTS certification process uses both flexible and standardized elements. Candidates for certification supply a videotape of their own lesson and do an analysis of their own instructional planning and decision making. These unique individual video elements are combined with common assessment center exercises, so NBPTS obtains a profile with both unique and shared elements.

SINGLE VERSUS MULTIPLE PURPOSES

Most of the assessment systems we reviewed were designed to serve primarily one of the three purposes discussed previously—i.e., to improve learning and instruction, to certify individual mastery, or to evaluate program success. For example, the NBPTS examinations are designed specifically to measure mastery of job-related knowledge and skills, rather than to diagnose skill deficiencies or evaluate the effectiveness of teacher education programs.

Our Oklahoma case, however, is one example of an assessment system designed to serve at least two purposes. Student scores are aggregated to the program level, where they are used by the state to monitor program effectiveness and contribute to funding decisions. In addition, scores are reported to teachers, who use them to identify weaknesses in their curriculum or instruction and to make adjustments. In some occupational areas, tests have a third purpose:

certifying students' competencies to increase their employment prospects in an occupation.

Although it is easy to differentiate the three purposes of assessment in the abstract, in reality they are interrelated. For example, knowing something about individual student progress through a unit offers some insight into the effectiveness of the program. In this sense, assessment results do not necessarily support only one use. However, information gathered with one purpose in mind is likely to be better suited to that purpose than to another. Certainly, aggregated or sampled scores that would be adequate for measuring changes at the program level are insufficient for monitoring changes at the individual level.

Some of the advantages of single-purpose versus multiple-purpose assessments are summarized in Table 13. One major advantage of a single-purpose assessment is that it can be made highly relevant to the needs of the users, leading to efficiencies in design, administration, and reporting. For example, when designing an assessment for program evaluation, it is possible to sample students and tasks rather than having all students complete all exercises. Sampling reduces the burden on participants while still providing trustworthy aggregate information for judging overall program effectiveness. However, this approach would not be appropriate for determining individual mastery, because each student does not respond to enough items to provide a valid score.

It is possible to design multipurpose assessments in theory, but it is difficult to do so in practice. One problem is that the size of the as-

Table 13

Advantages of Single Versus Multiple Purposes

Single Purpose	Multiple Purposes
Greater clarity in design, administration, and reporting of information	Greater efficiency in use of assessment resources
Less conflict between competing demands	More data sharing among users
Shorter and more focused assessments	

sessment increases as the number of purposes increases. Another problem is that different purposes can lead to conflicting demands. The Oklahoma assessment is used for both program accountability and student learning. These two uses are complementary, but there are some tensions between them that have to be resolved. For example, although Oklahoma provides common curriculum handbooks, not all teachers use them, with the result that some teachers and students do not view the test as complementary to their curriculum. They thus see the test as serving state reporting purposes but having little direct value to them.

Similarly, an assessment designed to provide individual diagnostic information needs to produce scores at a finer level of aggregation than a test that does not have to help students and teachers plan instruction. For example, one might need to know whether students have learned specific grammatical conventions as a basis for instructional planning—should the class review the use of apostrophes in the possessive form? However, in a program evaluation setting, it probably is adequate to sample a variety of grammatical conventions within a written communication task.

On the other hand, there are potential advantages to assessment systems that serve multiple purposes. If the technical difficulties can be overcome, a single assessment system is more efficient than multiple assessments in terms of resources and testing time. In the ideal case, a common broad assessment could produce a core database from which information could be extracted to address different questions. One potential advantage of a multipurpose assessment system is improved communication among stakeholders who would share common terms, references, and results. Another potential advantage is that it might generate greater support among policy makers responsible for funding the assessment. McDonnell (1994) describes differences among stakeholders' views of assessment, and points out that coalitions can sometimes be built if policy makers believe an assessment can support multiple goals.

VOLUNTARY VERSUS MANDATORY PARTICIPATION

One important element in the assessments conducted by Laborers-AGC, VICA, and NBTPS is that test-takers participate voluntarily. The alternative is to require that all eligible individuals sit for the tests, as is done in state testing programs such as KIRIS and Oklahoma.

Table 14 illustrates some of the advantages associated with voluntary versus mandatory participation. Students and teachers who participate in voluntary rather than compulsory testing programs are often more motivated to do well because they have made a commitment to the outcome. If, in their desire to be successful, they pay more attention to the tasks, focus their energies, and make more efficient use of time, the validity of the assessment results may even be increased. Voluntary participation may also increase the value of the assessment as a signaling tool because students and staff who choose to participate attend to it more. Teachers may adjust their curriculum based on student scores, and students may change their study habits. The assessment may have greater utility as a lever for reform because it is given greater credence by program participants. Increased attention may also enhance the educational value of the assessment experience itself. Finally, those who choose to participate often are more engaged in the learning experience than those whose participation is compelled.

But there are also advantages to required participation. Oklahoma, KIRIS, and C-TAP can be motivating because they are required. Teachers may attend to the content covered by the tests because all students are required to take them, although the degree of influence may be a result more of the consequences than of the level of participation (see discussion of high versus low stakes, above). Required assessments affect all participants, so whatever value is obtained accrues to everyone, not just the self-selected few. In

Table 14

Advantages of Voluntary Versus Mandatory Participation

Voluntary	Mandatory
Greater commitment from users, increasing likelihood that	Benefits of assessment affect everyone
• optimum performance is elicited (validity) • curriculum and instruction are influenced • users learn from participation	More widespread influence on curriculum and instruction Greater comparability across units

addition, assessment results are more likely to be useful for comparison across program units when all students participate. This is essential if the assessment is to be used for accountability purposes.

In most instances, program developers have little control over this aspect of assessment. The program context dictates whether testing is mandatory or not. However, there are cases in which design decisions can affect the amount of testing required of individuals and the way scores are used, which indirectly affects the emotional and psychological aspects of participation. For example, some state testing programs report scores on every student, which necessitates that every student complete the full test. Other states report only aggregate scores (e.g., at the classroom, school, or district level), which permits them to use matrix or item sampling. While all students must participate, each takes far fewer items, lessening some of the negative associations that accompany extended testing programs. In some instances, e.g., in Kentucky, a sample of students is selected for participation in the performance events, reducing further the perceived burden and giving participation an aura of specialness.

Chapter Six

DISCUSSION

Our project was undertaken to investigate the utility of alternative assessments for vocational education and to provide vocational educators with guidance in evaluating different strategies for assessment. The case studies provide a rich set of illustrations of the range of constructed-response measures that are available to vocational educators and the purposes they might serve. However, the cases do not identify a set of best practices or a simple formula for choosing among alternatives. Instead, our research suggests that vocational educators must make their own choices from a growing range of options. That information may be interpreted as either bad or good news. Some may long for a simple all-purpose solution; for them, the results of this study will be disappointing. Others may be excited to learn that they have considerable freedom to craft assessment systems to meet their needs.

Our project will have value if it helps vocational educators make better assessment choices. To that end, we have discussed a number of elements that need to be factored into assessment decisions. The choice of an assessment strategy should depend on the purposes to be served, the quality of the information desired, and the feasibility of different alternatives within the local context. Our six case studies illustrate how different programs have crafted assessment systems to meet specific needs. In addition, these case studies suggest a number of other factors educators must address when thinking about assessment systems.

The goal of the first two sections in this chapter is to illustrate how the information from the previous chapters might be used to address the needs of vocational educators. Two common situations—assessment for program improvement and assessment for certifying student mastery—are used to show how assessment planning can be informed by the results of our study. The last section then provides conclusions.

EXAMPLE: DEVELOPING ASSESSMENTS FOR PROGRAM IMPROVEMENT[1]

Dale McIver's Problem

Dale McIver teaches in the office automation program at Watson Tech, an area vocational technical school in Dade County, Florida. She teaches a three-course sequence leading to a certificate in office machine operation, but few of her students complete the full sequence. Instead, her classes are primarily composed of students wanting to gain some initial familiarity with computerized text and data processing or wanting to upgrade their skills in particular ways. Dale is frustrated with her current grading system, which is based on unit tests from the class workbooks. The test scores do not give her or the students enough information about the students' abilities to respond to realistic office demands that involve automated equipment. She is looking for an assessment system that will engage her students more, help them understand their own strengths and weaknesses, and provide her with information to improve her instruction. She believes there is too much emphasis on rote learning of commands and functions. She wants her students to be better problem solvers when it comes to using computers in the office environment.

Developing a Solution to Dale's Problem

Dale's situation should be familiar to vocational educators because the changes she is experiencing are widespread. In fact, part of the motivation for this project was to address these new challenges facing vocational educators. Our approach to solving Dale's problem

---

[1]The individuals, schools, and programs in this example and the one that follows are fictitious.

was to review the various assessment options in relation both to her purposes and to the quality and feasibility issues discussed earlier.

In this situation, the broad purpose for the assessment is unambiguous. Dale's interest is in improving the courses she teaches. She wants information to help students focus their efforts and to help her determine which skills need additional emphasis. She also recognizes there have been changes in the nature of the skills to be taught and the needs of the students who are enrolling, and she hopes the assessments will be responsive to these conditions. In particular, she wants information about how well students would respond to realistic problems.

All of the alternative assessment methods we have described could be used in this situation. Students could write extended descriptions of the procedures they would use in a particular office situation. Dale could develop realistic office tasks for students to perform and then judge their products. A course-long project culminating in a formal presentation is a possibility, but it seems less suitable than the other alternatives. A portfolio containing a collection of student products would work well. If part of Dale's goal is for students to build a repertoire of solution strategies and a command of the technology, then a collection of successful products might be a good contribution.

It is important to recall Dale's purpose and to consider how well each type of assessment would help the students and Dale to improve. We cannot analyze the situation completely without a clearer understanding of the type of problem-solving skills Dale hopes to foster and how well they can be embodied in the assessment. For example, does she expect students to be able to revise a document based on editor's marks, produce a presentation-quality organizational chart based on a sketch, or compile a report that includes text, tables, and a graph? Does she expect students to find a file without knowing its filename, recover a document after a power outage, or repair a faulty disk drive? These are all problems one might encounter in an office setting, but their solution requires different knowledge and skills. Some problem-solving abilities might be measured adequately with written questions, others with performance tasks, and others through an extended project.

Dale's plans for grading also play a role in selecting an assessment. Is the manner in which students produce the product important, or just the quality of the result? Some grading standards may be more helpful than others, just as certain types of feedback may be more informative than others. Dale knows (or can find out) the answers to these questions, so she can factor them into her evaluation of alternatives.

One of Dale's purposes for the assessment is program improvement. If it is to improve her courses, the assessment must provide information that is easy to link to instruction (either to particular units or to behaviors). Will Dale know what to do if students do poorly on one aspect of the assessment?

In Dale's case, it is not necessary to place a premium on technical quality. Students will have multiple opportunities to perform in class, and the assessment results will not be used for critical decisions. Dale need not be overly concerned about the accuracy of scoring. Teachers make judgments about student performance all the time, and there is no reason to think Dale will be unable to judge the responses to the assessment tasks fairly. In addition, if the results are going to be used to help students judge their own skills and to inform changes in lessons, validity is not of great importance. However, if Dale wants to draw inferences about broader behavior, such as problem solving in the office environment, she will need to collect far more information to test their validity.

All the alternatives are feasible, but each will increase the burden on Dale's time compared to her current assessment methods. None of the options involves great financial costs, but Dale will have to be willing to bear added preparation burdens. The portfolio appears to be the most demanding because of the time needed to organize it and assess the products at the end of the term. None of the alternatives appears to be so complex that Dale will need specialized help, or so unusual that she will encounter resistance from students or faculty.

Administrative issues are less germane to this situation. The vignette does not clarify whether Dale's problem is unique to her or shared by other teachers in the district. It might be possible to share the development effort with other office-automation teachers, so long as all remained engaged and committed to the work.

Some of the other factors discussed in Chapter Five come into play as well. The choice of single versus multiple types of assessment should probably be made after clarifying the kinds of problems students need to solve. It may be that a series of similarly organized scenarios can capture the desired problem-solving skills well. If the assessments reflect the course goals, then Dale will probably want to make them mandatory and give them considerable weight in determining course grades. Again, because the assessment is supposed to be closely linked to course expectations, it might be possible to embed it into class lessons in a relatively seamless way.

EXAMPLE: DEVELOPING ASSESSMENTS FOR CERTIFICATION

J.C. San Martino's Problem

J.C. San Martino is the coordinator of the automotive repair program for the Fort Meede School District. He supervises seven teachers in five high schools and one vocational school. Historically, the program has been very successful in preparing students for entry-level jobs in service stations and repair shops. In the past two or three years, however, local employers in various parts of the district have complained that graduates are not as good as they used to be. It has been hard for J.C. to respond, because the complaints are all different, but the common thread seems to be that students are very good at some things but have gaps in their training. Employers are losing confidence in the district's program, and they are growing cautious about hiring graduates. Although every school uses the same curriculum and teaches to the same set of competencies, each instructor is responsible for his or her own testing and grading. J.C. thinks that a common assessment system might help him raise standards in the program, assure employers that graduates are competent, and encourage instructors to provide more consistent training. He has considered offering employers a guarantee that graduates from the auto repair program will meet agreed-upon standards, but is not certain he could develop a system that would support this claim. He also wants to be sure that the assessment system provides information to help teachers improve their programs.

Developing a Solution to J.C.'s Problem

Comments from employers have led J.C. to question the quality and consistency of the training being provided in the district. He wants to use assessment to certify student competence, but he realizes that he must also provide information for program improvement or he will never achieve the certification goal. The problem is complicated by the fact that there appear to be problems with the individual schools, as well as with the overall program. So the assessment system needs to provide information to certify mastery and to identify shortcomings in the instructional program at each location.

More than one type of assessment can address J.C.'s concerns, but not all the approaches described in Chapter Three are equally helpful. Because the auto repair program is organized around a set of competencies and because employers have expressed concerns about specific skills, the assessment should relate to these specific program elements. Written tests and performance tasks can both be useful in this regard. Senior projects are less helpful for providing information about specific learning outcomes. Portfolios might be useful if constructed such that they contain information linked to core competencies and skills.

One issue J.C. must address before designing the assessment system is whether the course curriculum is aligned with the needs of local employers. It might be that the demands of entry-level auto repair jobs have changed in the past few years and the curriculum itself needs to be updated. Students may need to acquire new skills, such as using new finishes or new application procedures, or they may need to be prepared to work in different arrangements, such as multiperson teams. Reaffirming the link between course content and employer needs is an important first step; it also provides an opportunity to involve business and industry representatives in the program.

There are many ways to measure the competencies students are being asked to master, and J.C.'s biggest challenge will be choosing methods that strike the right balance between quality and feasibility. Strictly speaking, the "guarantee" he hopes to give to employers is not a binding contract, and there is no reason to apply the same quality standards one would apply to a licensing examination designed to protect public health and safety. Nevertheless, J.C. wants the effort to have merit, and he is particularly concerned about the consistency of performance across schools. It is not enough for each instructor to check off each competency as it is mastered; J.C. wants to impose some common external measures that have credibility with employers. Therefore, he may want to use common written exams to test knowledge, coupled with common performance tasks to measure some applied skills. Using the same scoring procedures for all schools will provide the comparability he desires, and assessment certainly should be mandatory for all students. This may also be an excellent opportunity to use industry representatives as judges to review student performance and provide external validation for the quality of the work. He should certainly investigate existing assessments that have been developed in conjunction with automotive industry organizations; it may not be necessary to develop new assessments if credible ones exist.

He must also keep in mind, however, that standardized measures (written or performance) require time and effort, and too much testing takes away from learning time and may annoy participants. Because there are many ways to measure competencies, it may make sense to measure some skills using quick and less intrusive methods (such as a checklist initialed by the instructor) and to measure other, more difficult or important skills using more time-consuming methods (such as standardized written tests or standardized performance assessments). In some cases, improvement may come from merely requiring students and instructors to monitor their progress against a master list of competencies. Requiring a portfolio in which students compile evidence of mastery of all course competencies is one alternative J.C. might consider.

It probably would be wise for J.C. to involve all the auto repair instructors in the development of the assessment system. This will help them understand the need for the system and increase their commitment to using it. More importantly, the instructors will have useful insights into ways to measure various skills, including those that may be difficult to measure (e.g., working in multiperson teams). For example, it may be possible to have embedded components in which existing class projects become the measurement tool for certain skills. Teachers also may have a better sense of the demands that certain choices will place on their time and the students' time. If the system is meaningful to instructors, it will increase the likelihood that they will participate enthusiastically. If instructors incorporate performance on the assessment into students' course grades, the system will have more meaning for students as well.

CONCLUSIONS

The results of our study indicate that alternative assessments can be useful tools for vocational education, but that vocational educators must learn to be wise consumers and users of assessments. Our examination of cases illustrates the breadth of assessment options available, from open-ended written assessments to performance tasks to portfolios. Each has been used effectively on a large scale in at least one location, and all appear to have potential for vocational education.

For vocational educators who do not know where to begin, we have suggested an approach for choosing among alternative assessments. The first step is to clarify the purposes of the assessment and the specific conditions of the vocational context. These conditions might include the needs of constituents, the demands for account- ability, and the nature of the skills to be assessed. Next, one should consider a wide range of assessment options. The case studies illus- trate a few alternatives that have been used in practice. Reading the complete descriptions in the appendices conveys a fuller picture of the demands of each situation and the strengths and weaknesses of the approaches taken. A thoughtful educator would supplement our findings with information from colleagues and professional organi- zations about other assessment methods that might be used or adapted.

Educators must also consider the issues of quality and feasibility. The manner in which the information will be used determines the level of technical quality that needs to be achieved. In general, the more importance attached to the use of the information, the higher the necessary levels of reliability and validity. However, quality con- cerns should be balanced against practical realities. Cost, time bur- dens, and acceptability by stakeholders are also important consid- erations in selecting assessment methods. Some approaches are cheaper, less intrusive, and more familiar than others.

In the end, no single assessment approach is best for all situations. However, fairly simple considerations can guide assessment planning. Our study illustrates the breadth of the existing alternative approaches, their utility in the vocational context, and some of the trade-offs vocational educators face when making choices among them.

CAREER-TECHNICAL ASSESSMENT PROGRAM

The Career-Technical Assessment Program (C-TAP) is a standards-based assessment system designed to support instruction of important career skills and assess the preparedness of California students for entry-level jobs and postsecondary educational training. The program was developed by WestEd, under the direction of the California Department of Education (CDE) and the Sacramento County Office of Education (SCOE), for use in vocational programs in California's high schools and regional occupational centers/programs. C-TAP assessments are being implemented in five career areas: agriculture, business, health careers, home economics, and industrial and technology education. Within each area, C-TAP is targeted either to clusters of occupations or a core program that teaches basic information relevant to a wider grouping of occupations. There are currently C-TAP assessment materials available for two clusters or core programs for each career area:

1. **Agriculture:** agriculture core, animal science

2. **Business:** marketing, computer science and information systems

3. **Health Careers:** health careers core, advanced core course

4. **Home Economics:** child development and education, food services and hospitality

5. **Industrial and Technology Education:** tech core, construction

DESCRIPTION AND PURPOSE

Originally, in 1990, C-TAP was planned as a set of specific occupational tests for over twenty-nine occupations. The tests were to be made up primarily of multiple-choice questions and some performance items measuring specific skills for entry-level jobs. C-TAP's primary purpose was to be a standardized statewide student certification system; its secondary purpose was to be a program evaluation tool.

C-TAP's purpose and content have changed over time. Early on, the focus switched from specific occupations and job skills to clusters of related occupations and broader skills, and expanded to include cumulative assessment components. Both shifts were consistent with other state and national initiatives in vocational education and assessment. C-TAP is currently being used primarily as a teaching/learning tool and as an assessment contributing to grades in vocational education programs. It is not yet widely used in any standardized fashion; rather, teachers tend to adapt the materials for use in their own classrooms. WestEd estimates that several hundred teachers are using C-TAP.

The C-TAP assessment system includes three components, each of which addresses academic skills, general workplace skills, and job-specific skills: (1) the portfolio, (2) the project, and (3) the written scenario. C-TAP is currently being expanded to include additional on-demand assessments (multiple choice and short written-response items) that will be administered by CDE. Each of the C-TAP assessment components is linked to California's career-technical model curriculum or challenge standards, as well as to related academic and career preparation standards. Scoring for the portfolios, projects, and written scenarios is done by teachers, using scoring rubrics designed by WestEd. Readers assign scores on specific dimensions of performance as well as an overall holistic score. There are four possible scoring levels: (1) Low Basic (incomplete and/or very unsatisfactory), (2) Basic (unsatisfactory), (3) Proficient (very good), and (4) Advanced (excellent).

The *portfolio* is a collection of student work that shows important knowledge, skills, and achievements. It serves as a vehicle for organizing and presenting students' work for assessment purposes, as well as for presentation to prospective employers or advanced training institutions. The portfolio contains five parts: an *introduction* (table of contents and letter of introduction), a *career development package* (an application for employment or college, a letter of recommendation, and a resume), *work samples* (at least four products in which the student illustrates mastery of specific skills as reflected in the model curriculum standards [MCS]), a w*riting sample* related to the student's career area, and a *supervised practical experience evaluation* (encouraged but not required, since career programs vary in their requirements for practical experience). Figure A.1 describes some portfolio work samples.

The *project* is a major piece of hands-on work requiring students to plan, develop, and evaluate an important product or event related to their career interests. The project includes four parts: (1) a *plan* out-

---

The work samples in the portfolio must document one or several specific technical skills and show the student's ability to communicate information about the skill. The samples usually combine written material and illustrations (drawings or photographs of physical artifacts the student created). Students also write a description of the work sample and explain the skills demonstrated. Examples:

> A student in a child development and education course designed a day care center as one of his work samples. The design included a floor plan of the center, a list of criteria to evaluate safety problems, a list of items to stock the center (including those needed to meet children's developmental needs), and each item's cost.

> A student in an animal science course documented how she gave a cow with mastitis an intramammary injection, using drawings, a picture of herself with the cow, and a written description of the procedure.

In a program for dental assistants, work samples have included documentation of how a student sterilizes instruments, takes a dental impression, pours a plaster mold, and takes a full set of x-rays.

Figure A.1—Examples of Work Samples from Portfolios

lining the process a student will go through to design and complete the project; (2) *evidence of progress* (a minimum of three pieces) showing the student's progress toward developing the final product; (3) a *final product/event*; and (4) an *oral presentation* in which the student describes his or her project, explains the standard-related knowledge and skills used, evaluates his or her own work, and explains what he or she learned. Figure A.2 describes some sample projects.

A student developed a travel brochure for Mexico as his project for a business course. First, he laid out a 12-step plan to develop the brochure and identified the resources necessary to implement the plan. As evidence of progress, he submitted a journal of his activities for developing the brochure, an interview protocol he used with travel agents, a data base of vacation hotels and their prices, and information on vacation spots located on the Internet. His final product was an eight-page brochure describing three vacation spots in Mexico (Los Cabos, Mazatlan, and Puerto Vallarta), bringing together the information he had supplied as evidence of progress.

A student in an agriculture core course reforested an area of marginal grazing land. First, he laid out a five-step plan and identified necessary resources. As evidence of progress, he submitted a journal that showed activities over four months, including land preparation, purchase of 200 trees, planting, and a site visit three months later to examine the trees. His final product was a photographic journal of the site, its preparation, and tree planting.

A student in a health careers course displayed the method of autopsy most commonly used by medical examiners. She set out a 14-step plan and list of resources. Her evidence of progress included a journal of activities, photos of herself and a partner drawing a model of a human torso, photos from a trip to a medical examiner's office, and an outline of information on autopsies. Her final product was three photos of a cadaver in various stages of an autopsy, with captions describing the stages, and a three-page written description of autopsy procedures.

Figure A.2—Sample Projects

Originally, C-TAP did not include a project but instead required an on-demand performance task (chosen centrally for all schools) and a separate oral presentation. When pilot tested, the on-demand task met with some opposition from teachers who felt it did not necessarily accommodate instructional and curricular differences among schools. As a result, the task and oral presentation were merged to create the project, which allows for some student choice and can be adapted to fit with the teacher's curriculum.

The *written scenario* is a forty-five-minute written response test that presents students with a "real-life" problem in their career area. Students must evaluate the problem and propose a means of addressing it. Their ability to demonstrate content knowledge is evaluated, as well as their problem-solving and communication skills. Scenarios were included in C-TAP to directly assess students' problem-solving skills. A scenario from a veterinary science class provides one example. Students read a description of an unhealthy cow's symptoms and living conditions. They then identify and write about the illnesses the cow may be suffering from, their causes, and possible treatment options.

C-TAP was recently expanded to include *multiple-choice and short written-response questions*. These on-demand components are designed to measure the breadth of students' career-technical knowledge. They will be administered and scored by CDE.

RELATIONSHIP TO OTHER PROGRAMS

In the future, C-TAP may continue its current form of usage while also fulfilling its originally intended role as part of a certification program. California has already incorporated it into certain reform initiatives. For example, California requires that eighty sites with tech-prep programs use C-TAP for assessing student progress. The state also is considering the use of certificates of initial and advanced mastery; if this initiative is adopted, C-TAP may become a requirement for the receipt of one or both certificates. Schools and programs that regularly use and score most C-TAP components can use it to develop their own certification system.

C-TAP is linked to several sets of state standards. The portfolio, project, and written scenario are tied to both career-technical model curriculum (content) standards (MCS) and career preparation (general workplace readiness) standards. There are separate MCS for each occupational cluster. The seven career preparation standards apply to all five career areas. The supervised practical experience evaluation in the portfolio specifically asks for students to be evaluated on these standards. The newly developed multiple-choice and short written-response items are linked to the draft interim content and performance standards, "Challenging Standards for Student Success," developed by CDE. There is substantial overlap between these standards and the career-technical MCS.

IMPLEMENTATION AND ADMINISTRATION

All of the teachers interviewed used the portfolio, which was generally deemed the strongest component of C-TAP. In turn, teachers saw the work samples as the most valuable element of the portfolio. Work samples require the student to document and explain what he or she has learned, which reinforces the material while also giving the student a record of his or her achievement for the future. This technique both bolsters students' self-esteem and provides evidence of knowledge and skills that can be shown to others.

Teachers believe that three types of skills are required for the portfolio: applied academic skills (especially writing), work readiness skills (demonstrated in the supervised practical experience evaluation and in how well the student communicates in the work samples), and specific technical skills. The requirements for the portfolio vary by program. For example, some teachers ask students to submit more work samples than the recommended four. The level of detail in work samples may vary greatly, e.g., from a half-page description of how to use a fax machine to several pages with photos describing how to vaccinate a lamb. The requirement for the writing sample also can take various forms, including a research paper written for a career-technical course, a paper related to a career-technical subject written in another course, and an expository paper describing a personal experience.

Teachers also differed in the weight they placed on C-TAP when evaluating students. All the teachers surveyed graded the subcomponents of the portfolio as well as the portfolio as a whole, placing primary emphasis on the work samples and writing sample. The contribution of the portfolio to students' final grades varied by teacher but reached as high as 80 percent. The majority also required the submission of a completed portfolio in order to pass the course or program, and one teacher tied a completed portfolio to receiving the career certificate plus college credit for the high school course. Where used, projects were graded. Scenarios were or were not graded, depending on the teacher.

The scenario and project components of C-TAP were used less consistently than the portfolio. Teachers gave several reasons for not using scenarios or projects, including the following: they created too much work when combined with portfolios; projects were already being assigned and evaluated, so C-TAP project materials added nothing new (or not enough that was new); and there were gaps between when particular material was taught and when the relevant scenarios arrived from WestEd. When teachers used projects, they often simply used the ideas provided in C-TAP to give more structure to an existing assignment. Use of the scenarios varied from once or twice during a course, to more often for practice, to once at the end of a unit.

TECHNICAL QUALITY

WestEd's attempts at determining the *reliability* of C-TAP have focused primarily on developing consistent scoring procedures. So far, this work has entailed selecting benchmarks and scoring student work, primarily for portfolios and scenarios. Benchmarks are examples of student work at the different performance levels (Low Basic, Basic, Proficient, and Advanced). They are used, along with training and calibration examples, to train teachers in how to score the products.

Portfolio Benchmarking and Scoring

As originally designed, the portfolio scoring process entailed two steps: (1) evaluating individual portfolio entries as students completed them and (2) reviewing and rating completed portfolios. Teachers were encouraged to give students feedback on the quality of their work throughout the portfolio development process to ensure they produced high-quality entries. Once all required entries were present, the portfolios were evaluated and assigned one holistic rating of Basic, Proficient, or Advanced.

The original C-TAP rating guide comprised four dimensions identified as critical for demonstrating competence in career-technical areas. These dimensions included *content* (breadth, depth, and application of knowledge and skills related to the career-technical MCS), *career preparation* (understanding of career preparation and personal employability attributes), *analysis* (ability to apply analytical skills to the gathering of information and the evaluation of one's own work), and *communication* (effective use of communication). The rating guide provided qualitative descriptions for each of the dimensions for the three performance levels (Basic, Proficient, and Advanced). Raters were asked to review a student's work, considering each of the evaluation dimensions. They were then required to assign one holistic score (Basic, Proficient, or Advanced) based on their overall impression of the student's work, all dimensions considered.

Benchmarking sessions were held in the summer of 1993 using the above process. Basic and proficient benchmarks were identified for the career-technical areas of animal science, child development and education, computer science and information systems, construction, and health careers core. The benchmarking session provided invaluable information that was used to refine the portfolio entries and requirements. However, as a result of these refinements, the benchmarks identified during the 1993 benchmarking session were not valid for subsequent years.

To give teachers and students time to adjust to the changes that were made, whole portfolios were not reviewed in 1994. In the summer of 1995, portfolios were evaluated by subject area. Sample portfolios that reflected proficient work were identified. Because these portfolios were to serve as exemplars for training, minor edits were made to assure clear adherence to portfolio requirements and performance standards.

During 1996, the holistic scoring method previously used to evaluate portfolios was reconsidered. Following a review of the results of several similar assessment efforts around the nation, a modified analytic approach was adopted to help ensure acceptable levels of reliability.

The modified method requires scorers to provide actual ratings for each of the dimensions before providing an overall holistic score, so a portfolio now receives multiple scores rather than just one. WestEd added this step to address two possible sources for error in the rating of student portfolios—variations due to student performance and scorer variability. The quality of student performance can vary across dimensions. By evaluating each of the dimensions separately, raters can note this uneven student performance. Raters can also show variability in the scores they assign to individual portfolios. Requiring separate dimensional scores allows for the comparison of scorers at the dimension as well as the holistic level.

The developers of C-TAP also hoped that the use of dimensional scores would yield instructional benefits. Holistic scores alone do not provide teachers or students with specific information about relative strengths and weaknesses. The dimensional scores help support and explain the overall holistic rating by identifying those dimensions in which a student is showing satisfactory or exemplary performance as well as those areas needing improvement. Dimensional scores also can be compared with other instructional and assessment indicators, e.g., classroom grades, test scores, and standardized test and subtest scores.

The new dimensional scoring guide for portfolios includes the same four dimensions described earlier with minor revisions, and adds a fifth dimension by separating knowledge and application of content knowledge into two distinct dimensions. Previous raters indicated that students may demonstrate technical knowledge, for example in a writing sample, but are not always able to demonstrate the ability to accurately apply that knowledge. This lack of continuity between knowledge and application led to the separation of these two dimensions.

In addition, a fourth performance level (Low Basic) was added for the dimensional ratings and the overall holistic judgment, so each of the dimensions is now delineated into four performance levels rather than three. The new performance level was included in direct response to requests from teachers who found that three levels did not adequately represent the range of student performance. They considered it important to distinguish students who failed to make a full attempt to meet the requirements of the portfolio (Low Basic) from students who extended the effort but did not achieve at the proficient level (Basic).

Project Scoring

Because of their somewhat limited use, projects did not require extensive scoring sessions like those held for portfolios and written scenarios. Instead, focused review and benchmarking sessions were conducted for the C-TAP project in 1994 and 1995. Both sessions involved teachers who had implemented the C-TAP project in their classrooms. In 1994, teachers were brought together with WestEd staff and CDE representatives to review projects and select benchmarks for each content area. In the summer of 1995, teachers, WestEd staff, and CDE representatives reviewed student projects and identified student work to serve as exemplars in the following career areas: agriculture core, animal science, computer science and information systems, marketing, health careers core, child development and education, food service and hospitality, technology core, and construction technology. These samples were edited as needed to assure strict adherence to the project guidelines and were disseminated statewide as examples of student work meeting the C-TAP project requirements for each content area.

In 1996, as with portfolios, a decision was made to move toward dimensional scoring of projects. New dimensional scoring guides were developed for the project and the associated oral presentation following a process similar to that used for the portfolio. WestEd is in the process of soliciting feedback on the revised scoring guides from teachers and others actively involved with the C-TAP project.

Scenario Scoring

Until the 1995–1996 academic school year, written scenarios were scored holistically, using a generic written scenario rating guide that was the same for all scenarios regardless of career area or occupational cluster. The rating guide consisted of three scoring dimensions: *content* (the breadth, depth, and application of knowledge of major ideas and concepts related to career-technical MCS), *analysis* (the evaluation of evidence presented in the scenario and quality of response to all instructions and requirements in the written scenario assessment task), and *communication* (the effective use of written communication). Using the holistic rating guide, scorers were asked to review student responses to a scenario, considering all three dimensions, and then assign a holistic score. When determining holistic scores, raters were told to give less weight to written communication than to the other two dimensions because the scenario was not designed to focus too heavily on written communication skills.

In 1996, a decision was made to use both a generic guide and item-specific guides for the scenario. The generic scoring guide used previously is now intended to facilitate the development of item-specific guides tailored to the individual requirements of each written scenario. This change was made because it was generally agreed that item-specific guides would provide more specific information to scorers, making judgments more objective and reliable.

Just as the portfolio and project moved toward dimensional scoring and a four-point scale in 1996, so did the written scenario. In the process of refining the generic and new item-specific guides to reflect these changes, project staff conducted a review of written scenario responses across various content areas and prompts. During this review, it became clear that specifying separate criteria for the dimensions of *content* and *analysis* was not meaningful. That is, staff found it difficult to tease out evidence of content knowledge/application versus analysis in a written scenario response. As a result, the written scenario guides were refined to encompass only two dimensions—*content and analysis* and *written communication*—instead of the original three.

To address *content validity*, WestEd established two committees of experts to advise on the type of performance assessments to include in the C-TAP system. These committees were influential in the initial decision to limit the use of multiple-choice questions. They also provided input into the structure of the portfolio and its contents.

The advisory committees were replaced by development committees, each focusing on a specific occupational cluster. These committees were made up primarily of career-technical teachers but also included academic subject teachers, postsecondary faculty, and employers. For the portfolio, these committees produced lists of topics for the writing sample and ideas for work samples. For the project, they generated sample project aims to reflect appropriate content and scope. The development committees also drafted written scenarios that WestEd staff revised and field tested.

Content validity was also examined using focus groups. These groups reviewed completed student work to determine whether it demonstrated the skills desired in the workplace. Although this process has been somewhat informal, the results have been positive. WestEd plans to establish more formal focus groups made up of employers, industry practitioners, teachers, and postsecondary educators in the relevant career fields. These focus groups will consider whether the current form of each component of C-TAP and its scoring process are valid assessments of career-technical knowledge and skills. No other validity work has been done, such as correlating C-TAP ratings with other student ratings (such as test scores or teacher ratings) or using C-TAP ratings to predict student performance based on particular criteria.

CONSEQUENCES AND USE OF ASSESSMENT RESULTS

Because C-TAP has not been used statewide as a formal student certification system, it has not been implemented in a standard manner at all schools. Teachers differ in their use of C-TAP components and in the importance they place on C-TAP work when evaluating students.

C-TAP, especially the portfolio, is intended to document students' knowledge and skills and has been promoted as a means of impressing employers and postsecondary institutions through evidence of student achievement. Some teachers are somewhat skeptical of the usefulness of C-TAP for these ends. They believe that postsecondary institutions are generally unwilling to use portfolios alone for making admissions decisions. One teacher did note, however, that colleges were more willing to give college credit for her high school course upon reviewing her students' portfolios. Perceptions of C-TAP's usefulness for job seeking were more mixed. Anecdotal evidence suggests that some employers are impressed by portfolios while others are not. Overall, teachers found it challenging to get employers to consider portfolios when hiring. Teachers, however, argue that having portfolios gives students examples of their work and accomplishments that can be shared and discussed with potential employ-ers who show interest. Where students do internships while taking classes, C-TAP may also generate employer interest. For example, a health teacher noted that several dentists asked for student interns who would be producing work samples as part of their internship.

The purpose of C-TAP is still evolving from the original idea of a stu-dent certification program. To different degrees in different schools, it has modified instruction, become a source of information for grading or a requirement for passing a class, and created a record of student work that may convince both a student and a prospective employer/admissions officer that the student has learned useful skills. WestEd is in the process of evaluating C-TAP's impact on in-struction and curriculum by surveying and interviewing teachers.

APPLICABILITY TO VOCATIONAL EDUCATION

C-TAP is a vocational assessment system, so the key question is whether it could be implemented on a widespread basis. This question is difficult to answer for two reasons. First, C-TAP has been adopted schoolwide in only a limited number of cases. Second, not all teachers surveyed had adopted all three components of C-TAP. Some argue that there is not enough time to do all three, and others say they will adopt the project and scenario only after they have become comfortable with the portfolio. There has also been some concern that scenarios would be used to evaluate teachers, because they were originally designed to be centrally scored. For these reasons, the focus here is solely on the feasibility of implementing C-TAP portfolios. Feasibility includes the effects of portfolio use on teacher time and responsibilities, plus the reactions of teachers, parents, students, and schools.

Teachers agreed that using the portfolio took substantial amounts of class time, especially in the first year. Much of the time went to ex-plaining what was expected and giving students adequate time to carry out certain parts of the portfolio that were not traditionally part of the class (e.g., resumes and letters of application). For most teachers, the work samples came from existing classroom activities, but extra time was still required for students to write summaries. Teachers did give up teaching some material to make time for the portfolios.

Additional instructional demands are placed on teachers who use the portfolios. They have to focus more on writing, especially specialized writing such as resumes and job/college applications. Additionally, class management skills play a role, because students complete work samples at different speeds. Grading does not appear to pose an additional burden when the portfolio is used to supplant traditional tests or practicals. In fact, teachers said portfolio grading was easier than the traditional type because it is obvious from work samples whether students understand the material. If traditional assessments are continued, however, C-TAP requires additional grading time.

A further demand on teachers is the need to create storage space for the portfolios. Portfolios can take up substantial amounts of classroom space, and they must be easily accessible to students. Some teachers want to keep all the work samples students have done in class rather than just those selected for the portfolio. Students can then change their portfolio contents as needed. Other teachers are trying to determine where to store portfolios that will be maintained over all the years students are in the program.

The teachers surveyed believe the portfolio is a valuable approach and see a reduced learning curve for other teachers who subsequently adopt it with some help. Some teachers have been involved in training large numbers of their colleagues in the portfolio's use and believe that teachers with different levels of experience will vary in their willingness to use it. New teachers, for example, may not have time to adopt portfolios, while older teachers, especially those near retirement, may not want to invest the time. They do not yet see strong support from school administrators for using the portfolios. Students seem to resist the additional work requirements of the portfolio, but over time they come to accept them. Some students value having the record of work when they approach employers. Teachers have given portfolios a fairly low profile as they learn to use them. For this reason, there has been little community response to them up to this point. Parents are generally not familiar with portfolios, but usually react favorably when teachers explain them.

In conclusion, widespread adoption of C-TAP portfolios by individual teachers appears to be feasible, if teachers can find time to learn how to use them and agree that substantive course material may have to be dropped, at least initially, to free up time for their use. WestEd is distributing the cluster-specific supplements (which contain the career-technical MCS, ideas for projects and writing samples, and an example of a work sample write-up) and the examples of proficient student work (each containing one portfolio or project and together covering the occupational clusters). Teachers and students can use these to gain a better understanding of how to implement C-TAP and what completed projects and portfolios should look like.

KENTUCKY INSTRUCTIONAL RESULTS
INFORMATION SYSTEM (KIRIS)

The Kentucky Instructional Results Information System (KIRIS) is a multidimensional measurement and assessment system that supports the statewide educational accountability system in Kentucky. It was initiated by the Kentucky Department of Education in 1991 in response to a comprehensive statewide educational reform law. KIRIS collects data on cognitive outcomes in grades 4, 8, and 12 and combines them into one accountability index for each school. Schools that achieve adequate gains on the index receive financial rewards; consistent failure triggers state intervention. The cognitive measures are primarily performance based; they include on-demand constructed-response questions and performance events, as well as portfolios.

Educators in the state report that KIRIS has had strong effects on curriculum and instruction. External evaluators invited by the legislature to review KIRIS raised serious concerns about the quality of the measures and their validity for the state's purposes. The Kentucky Department of Education has made many changes to the system in response to these concerns, and additional changes were being considered at the time of this writing. KIRIS is the first example of a strong statewide accountability system built on performance measures that has been implemented, and it has interesting lessons for all educators.

DESCRIPTION AND PURPOSE

The Kentucky Educational Reform Act of 1990 (KERA) represented a dramatic reform of the state's educational system, with a strong emphasis on accountability. KERA embodied a particular approach to education in that it

- Set goals for the educational system.

- Created a mechanism for assessing progress toward those goals.

- Established rewards and sanctions for schools based on performance.

Figure B.1 lists the six major goals that were set for learners in the areas of basic communication and mathematics skills; application of concepts and principles to real-life situations; self-sufficiency; school attendance; school dropout/ retention rates; elimination of barriers to learning; and transitioning from high school to work, further

---

1. Students are able to use basic communication and mathematics skills for purposes and situations they will encounter throughout their lives.

2. Students shall develop their abilities to apply core concepts and principles from mathematics, the sciences, the arts, the humanities, social studies, practical living studies, and vocational studies to what they will encounter throughout their lives.

3. Students shall develop their abilities to become self-sufficient individuals.

4. Students shall develop their abilities to become responsible members of a family, work group, or community, including demonstrating effectiveness in community service.

5. Students shall develop their abilities to think and solve problems in a variety of situations they will encounter in life.

6. Students shall develop their abilities to connect and integrate experiences and new knowledge from all subject matter fields with what they have previously learned, and build on past learning experiences to acquire new information through media sources.

Figure B.1—Kentucky's Six Learner Goals

education, or the military (Kentucky Department of Education, 1993). Schools are the basic unit used to measure performance in Kentucky. The state expects schools to steadily improve their performance relative to these six goals.

The Kentucky Department of Education was charged with creating a system to measure and report school performance against these goals; KIRIS was the result. KIRIS scores are made up of two components, noncognitive and cognitive measures. The noncognitive measures account for about 16 percent of the total score for a school and include attendance, retention, dropout, and transition rates. The cognitive measures, which are collected only in grades 4, 8, and 12, cover the core academic subjects (mathematics, reading, science, social studies, writing, humanities and the arts) and practical living and vocational studies. Standards for performance have been set for the cognitive measures, and student work is classified into one of four performance levels: Novice, Apprentice, Proficient, or Distinguished.

The cognitive measures, which are primarily performance based,[1] originally included open-ended items, performance events, and portfolios (Kentucky Department of Education, 1995a). The open-ended items are in both the short-answer and the essay format. Performance events, which last about one class period, include some group work followed by individual work leading to an individual written product. They are administered on a matrix-sampled basis, with each student working on just one or two events. Portfolios are collected in writing and mathematics; each one contains five to seven "best pieces" of student work that cover different content areas and different core concepts. There are no content requirements for the portfolios, but they are supposed to demonstrate breadth as well as higher-order skills in each domain.

Measures from all domains (cognitive and noncognitive) are combined into a single accountability index for each school. The relative weights assigned to the content areas for the next cycle of accountability are summarized in Table B.1. A baseline index was computed using 1991–1992 performance, and an improvement target was

---

[1]From 1991–1992 to 1993–1994, the number of multiple-choice items was cut in half and the number of open-response items was doubled.

Table B.1

Index Weights for Next Cycle of Accountability

Content Area	Weight (%)
Mathematics	14
Reading	14
Science	14
Social studies	14
Writing	14
Arts and humanities	7
Practical living/vocational studies	7
Noncognitive index	16

established using this score.[2] (Greater gains on the baseline index are expected for low-scoring schools than for high-scoring schools.) Subsequent biennial averages are used as baselines for future improvement targets. Kentucky's long-term goal over a twenty-year period is that all schools will score above the 100 level (which is equivalent to having all students at the Proficient level).

Kentucky has a strong commitment to inclusion, and very few students are excluded from participation in the assessment. Special-education students complete an alternative portfolio based on their individual educational plans. Scores from these students are included in the computation of the school's accountability index.

RELATIONSHIP TO OTHER PROGRAMS

KERA created the framework for a new educational system incorporating the six goals shown in Figure B.1. KIRIS is the measurement and accountability system created to support KERA. KIRIS is seen as one part of the "complex network intended to help schools focus their energies on dramatic improvement in student learning" (Kentucky Department of Education, 1995b, p. 2). The state's goal is to create an integrated program of assessment, accountability, curriculum reform, and staff support. Because there are high stakes at-

---

[2]Recently, changes were made to improve the technical quality of KIRIS scores. For example, performance events are no longer included in the accountability index.

tached to performance, education officials expect to observe "teaching to the test," so they have tried to design an assessment system based on events worth "teaching to."

In accordance with KERA, KIRIS was built to assess school performance against the six broad learner goals shown in Figure B.1. KERA also required the department of education to create a performance-based assessment program to measure success. Goals 1, 2, 5, and 6 address the application of cognitive skills, and the contractor responsible for developing KIRIS worked with educators in Kentucky to develop assessments that measured these cognitive outcomes. The learner goals themselves are too broad to serve as test specifications, so in 1991 the Kentucky Board of Education adopted a more detailed set of valued outcomes that described in greater detail the skills learners should possess in the fields of mathematics, science, art, humanities, social studies, practical living, and vocational studies.

For the next two years, these outcomes were used as the basis for developing assessment tasks. However, these outcomes proved to be confusing to many important audiences, including parents, and were replaced by a set of fifty-seven "academic expectations" describing what Kentucky students should know and be able to do when they graduate from high school. Subsequent KIRIS assessment development has focused on these academic expectations (Kentucky Department of Education, 1995b).

KIRIS was built to assess school performance in response to broad new demands placed on education. The associated outcomes or expectations were derived by panels of educators to reflect this new direction, not existing programs. In particular, the vocational outcomes are quite general and do not necessarily match with the objectives of specific vocational programs. Only three of the fifty-seven academic outcomes relate to vocational studies:

- Students use strategies for choosing and preparing for a career.

- Students demonstrate skills and work habits that lead to success in future schooling and work.

- Students demonstrate skills such as interviewing, writing resumes, and completing applications that are needed to be accepted into college or other postsecondary training, or to get a job.

KIRIS is not focused specifically on assessing learning in vocational classes. In both 1992–1993 and 1993–1994, only three performance events and eleven open-response items per grade level were used to assess practical living and vocational studies combined, and this content area counted for only 7 percent of the overall accountability index (Kentucky Department of Education, 1995b). Most students completed only one performance event and one open-response item in this domain. This does not provide enough information to be useful for evaluating vocational programs, either at the individual or program level. Over time, one might expect to see greater coordination between specific instructional activities and the statewide assessment. Furthermore, the career skills measured by KIRIS might be useful indicators of one aspect of vocational education. However, as presently conceived, KIRIS itself will not be sufficient for evaluating specific vocational programs. Rather, vocational educators may be able to learn about performance-based accountability systems from the KIRIS model.

IMPLEMENTATION AND ADMINISTRATION

Kentucky has supported the implementation of KIRIS with extensive teacher training and technical assistance (Kentucky Department of Education, 1993). It established eight regional service centers to train district staff as associates, whose role is to help their districts further professional development. Districts and schools report that the centers are a valuable resource. The department of education funded a program to train KERA assessment fellows, whose role is to be available throughout the state to help schools and districts prepare for and interpret KIRIS; over 300 educators have participated in this program. Over 100 teachers have been trained as Distinguished educators, their function being to help schools succeed (particularly those whose scores are low). The Kentucky educational television network has broadcast fourteen professional development sessions. In addition, colleges and universities in Kentucky have offered courses and contracted with individual districts to train teachers in the new assessment methods and other aspects of KERA school reform.

The contractor responsible for KIRIS has trained 700 people as mathematics portfolio cluster leaders to help teachers in their area understand the portfolio guidelines and implement appropriate classroom procedures. Over 1,000 teachers have participated in guided scoring practice workshops for the writing portfolios. Teachers also have been involved in summer scoring of portfolios, which they report is beneficial for their professional development. Overall, the state has engaged in a broad and thorough effort to provide information and training to prepare teachers for the new assessment and accountability system.

Kentucky contracted with Advanced Systems in Measurement and Education (ASME) to develop and administer KIRIS. ASME worked closely with teams of Kentucky educators to formulate plans for the assessment, develop test items and open-response tests, administer the performance events, score the assessments, and set standards for student performance. ASME, in turn, contracted with WestEd for collection and analysis of the noncognitive data on attendance, retention, dropout, and transition rates.

It is difficult to estimate the total cost of KIRIS. The contractor receives about $6 million per year for developing the assessments, administering them, scoring the results, and reporting to schools and the state. This funding also covers some staff development activities. The Kentucky Department of Education also spends about $2 million a year on professional development of this type for teachers. In addition, some districts contract separately with ASME for additional scoring for continuous assessment, and the annual budget for rewards to schools is estimated to be about $18 million (Kentucky Institute for Education Research, 1995).

In addition, the KIRIS assessment requires school time. Each student completes four periods of on-demand assessment (periods were ninety minutes long in grades 8 and 12, and sixty minutes long in grade 4). If students need additional time, they are given a half-period more to complete the activities. Each student also devotes one period to a performance event, administered at the school by ASME staff. Writing and mathematics portfolios are collected throughout the year, but we were unable to find an estimate of the additional time spent preparing the portfolios (above and beyond the time required to do the assignments).

Teachers also devote some school time to preparing for KIRIS, but whether this is a cost or a benefit depends on the nature of the activities. KIRIS is designed to promote changes in curriculum and instruction, and, in theory, the time schools devote to preparing for KIRIS can be considered instructional time. Surveys administered by RAND suggest that teachers put considerable time into test preparation (Koretz, Mitchell, Barron, and Stecher, 1996). However, there is little evidence indicating whether this is appropriate preparation (activities that promote improvement in the broad domain of skills measured by KIRIS) or inappropriate preparation (time spent narrowly preparing students for specific KIRIS tasks or activities that might not generalize beyond the particular content of the test).

TECHNICAL QUALITY

In 1994, a panel of distinguished measurement specialists was appointed to investigate the technical quality of KIRIS. Their specific charge was to determine whether the accountability index was sufficiently robust to support how it was being used. The panel concluded that KIRIS is "significantly flawed and needs to be substantially revised" (Hambleton et al., 1995, Exec. Summary, p. 1), and it made fourteen recommendations for improving the system. The panel members were particularly concerned that the public was being misinformed "about the extent to which student achievement has improved" and about the "accomplishment of individual students" (ibid, p. 5).

The panel based its conclusion on evidence relating to six aspects of KIRIS, all of which are important considerations in the use of alternative assessments in vocational education. Each is discussed briefly in the following paragraphs, much of the discussion adapted directly from Hambleton et al. (1995).[3]

---

[3]In 1995–1996, the Kentucky Department of Education and its assessment contractor implemented all of the evaluation panel's recommendations with the exception of eliminating the writing portfolios. Analysis of the 1995–1996 writing portfolios showed continued improvement in scoring reliability and accuracy.

Assessment Development Process

The greatest weakness that the panel found in the development and documentation process was that the specifications (frameworks) do not communicate clearly what students are expected to know and be able to do, and therefore do not provide adequate signals to teachers and test developers. Since the test emphasizes cross-cutting themes rather than traditional discipline-based knowledge, an understanding of the exact nature of the expectations is important. In Kentucky, the test frameworks vary in detail and specificity across subjects, and frequently they do not contain any information about variations in expected student performance across grade levels. It is important to note that the greatest weaknesses in this area were found in the first year, and the process has been improving since then.[4] The panel was also critical of the process that was used to develop assessments, recommending that the state clearly follow four steps: specify goals explicitly, construct exercises that measure progress toward these goals, evaluate the exercises by having judges examine pilot-test results from students, and select and assemble test forms using acceptable items.

Accountability Index

A second problem was that the scores reported for schools did not have adequate reliability for accountability purposes: the scores reported for students were less reliable than the usual standard for such tests. The panel concluded that a substantial number of schools probably were assigned to the wrong reward category (Eligible for Reward, Successful, Improving, Decline, In Crisis), and that such errors of assignment were particularly likely for small schools. Furthermore, there was inadequate information to determine the likely level of error due to differences in task sampling from year to year, so the problems the panel was able to identify probably underestimated the true error of classification. Another problem was that student score reports did not convey information about the margin of error of reported scores, which should be included,

---

[4]Unfortunately, scores from the first year helped to establish each school's baseline performance level, so the initial weak test development process affected later rewards and sanctions.

according to accepted test standards (American Psychological Association, 1985). The panel noted that reliability of both student scores and school scores (i.e., information used for assessment purposes and for accountability purposes) could be improved by using both multiple-choice and open-response tasks to obtain scores, an option that was rejected by Kentucky in its commitment to emphasize performance assessment.

Portfolio Scoring Procedures

The panel examined separately the scores generated by the portfolio component of KIRIS, reporting negative findings about the reliability and validity of these scores as well. It is important to remember that the Kentucky portfolios served dual purposes: to provide measures of student achievement for the accountability system and to encourage changes in curriculum and instruction. On the first point, the panel found that scores were insufficiently reliable to support their use for accountability. Specifically, although raters were moderately consistent in ranking student work, they disagreed about the percentage of portfolios reaching each of the KIRIS performance levels. More damning was the fact that ratings by students' own teachers were higher than ratings by independent judges.

There was little evidence available about the validity of scores, but the panel was particularly concerned about the lack of standardization in the way portfolio entries are produced and the amount of assistance students receive. (This is a problem that undermines the validity of portfolio scores in other states as well.) Another problem of interpretation is that portfolios constructed of "best pieces" may not reflect sustainable levels of performance under normal conditions. The panel was more optimistic about the potentially beneficial effects of the portfolios on curriculum and instruction. Little information had been gathered about instructional impact at the time of the review, but, based on evidence from other portfolio assessment systems, the panel encouraged Kentucky to maintain the system on a low-stakes basis while gathering evidence about its long-term effects on classrooms.

Making Scores Comparable Across Years (Equating)

Next, the panel tackled the difficult question of the comparability of scores over time. KIRIS allocates rewards and sanctions on the basis of comparisons between performance in baseline years and subsequent years. Therefore, it is essential that the scores be comparable from one administration to the next even though the tasks, events, and items may vary. Although much of the panel's analysis was highly technical, involving the appropriate statistical equating designs, its conclusions were clear: the equating process was insufficient. KIRIS used too many judgmental procedures without adequate standardization, particularly in the translation from raw scores to performance levels. This introduced errors into the year-to-year comparisons. Other problems that undermined the equating of scores from year to year included changes in procedures and the exclusion of multiple-choice items (which have higher reliability) from the accountability index. Overall, the panel found that the equating did not support year-to-year comparisons, and it recommended a number of changes to strengthen the process.

Setting Performance Standards

Classification of students into proficiency levels is at the core of KIRIS, and the accuracy of these classifications affects the accuracy of each school's accountability index. Students are classified as Novice, Apprentice, Proficient, or Distinguished on each assessment, based on their scores. The assignment of scores to proficiency levels is done through judgmental processes in which panels review student responses and classify them according to descriptions of performance at the four levels. The investigatory panel found that these processes were not adequately described and appeared to lack appropriate standardization. It particularly criticized the standard-setting process, which at times assigned students to a proficiency level on the basis of as few as three test items.

Impact on Student Learning

Finally, the panel looked at the evidence of educational improvement in Kentucky; in other words, Has KIRIS had the desired effects on student performance? The Kentucky Department of Education trumpeted the improvement in student scores from 1991–1992 to 1993–1994, and the general public was led to believe that substantial progress had been made. The panel tried to determine to what extent these score changes reflect real differences in student learning. It concluded that the reported gains "substantially over-state improvements in student achievement" (Hambleton et al., 1995, sec. 8, p. 2). Panel members based this judgment on external evidence on student performance, such as NAEP, which does not show any improvement over the same time period (although there is a limit to how many such comparisons can be made at the same grade level and for the same subject). Though the panel members could not explain the differences, they suggested that inflated gains were attributable to two factors: the high stakes attached to KIRIS led to inappropriate teaching to the test, and the desire to show big increases in scores led to overly poor performance during the baseline year.

CONSEQUENCES AND USE OF ASSESSMENT RESULTS

The accountability index was used for the first time in 1994 to reward and sanction schools. Each school received a detailed report of its students' performance and its overall accountability index. Additional money was awarded to schools that met the threshold for rewards. The reports have been used in a variety of ways that are "consistent with the intent of KIRIS" (Kentucky Department of Education, 1995b, p. 222), including to monitor the progress of programs over time and to target instructional program improve-ment efforts.

KERA and KIRIS have had broad effects on curriculum assessment and professional development. There is clear evidence that some teachers are changing instructional practices in response to KIRIS as-sessment content and processes. For example, the use of writing portfolios has led to an increased emphasis on student writing. However, there is evidence that teachers are lagging in reforming many practices, including some assessment-related ones. They "are struggling with the use of learning centers and theme-centered units; are failing to use recommended practices in science, social studies and the arts; are not planning their instructional program around

Kentucky's Learning Goals and Academic Expectations; are having difficulty implementing a variety of continuous, authentic assessments; are neglecting to plan with special area teachers; and [are] failing to involve parents in the primary program" (Kentucky Institute for Education Research, 1994, pp. xvii–xviii).

APPLICABILITY TO VOCATIONAL EDUCATION

Much can be learned from KIRIS that has value for vocational education. On the positive side, some of the changes that proved most difficult for Kentucky educators should be relatively easy for vocational educators already accustomed to using performance as a basis for assessment. Similarly, the development of clear descriptions of desired outcomes and student proficiencies that has proved so difficult in Kentucky is very akin to the task analyses common in vocational education and so should create fewer problems. When vocational educators try to design assessments to measure unfamiliar skills and performances (e.g., generic skills, such as teamwork or understanding of systems), they will face similar problems of definition and communication, but their experience with task delineation and performance specification should stand them in good stead.

On the negative side, strong accountability requirements seem to make most aspects of assessment more difficult. Greater resources will be needed for everything from development to training to implementation if such an assessment is used to structure an accountability system.

Not one of the assessment elements of KIRIS is new; other testing programs use portfolios, performance events, and open-ended responses, and other states produce school "report cards" with indicators of both cognitive and noncognitive outcomes. What is unique about KIRIS is the use of these measures in a strong accountability context. The presence of high stakes exacerbates the political problems, raises the necessary technical standards, and heightens the anxiety level of educators, all of which would make it difficult to implement KIRIS-like assessments in similar contexts. The use of a single summary index of performance without the high stakes might be beneficial for some purposes, however.

Of particular concern is the need for high-quality measurement, a goal that still eludes KIRIS after four years (according to the technical experts). Such quality standards increase the time and resources needed for all aspects of the assessment, including developing student outcome goals, producing assessment specifications, developing tasks, scoring student responses, setting standards, equating forms, and reporting. These types of technical issues must be confronted by vocational educators if they want to use performance assessment for certifying competency, awarding certificates of mastery, or other important ends. In fact, the technical demands will be greater if the assessments are going to be used to make decisions about individuals. The KIRIS experience suggests that such an approach will require advanced technical expertise as well as considerable time and resources. Despite the criticisms of KIRIS, political support for educational improvement continues in Kentucky, as do efforts to improve the accountability system.

LABORERS-AGC ENVIRONMENTAL TRAINING AND CERTIFICATION PROGRAMS

In 1969, the Laborers International Union of North America and the Associated General Contractors of America (AGC) established a co-operative trust fund for the common purpose of improving the skills of construction laborers. The union sought to increase the demand for its workers, the contractors wanted more productive craft workers, and both parties had a vested interest in creating safer workplaces. For the last twenty-six years, the Laborers-AGC Education and Training Fund has been meeting these goals by developing and supporting occupationally focused courses for sixty-six affiliated local training schools in the United States and Canada. These schools are responsible for training the 350,000 union members (half of the membership) who work in construction or environmental cleanup. More than half of the schools (forty) offer environmental courses in addition to construction courses. Contractors pay money into local trust funds, which pay for running the affiliated schools and help defray Laborers-AGC's costs for curriculum and assessment development and technical support.

The first fifteen years of the fund's efforts concentrated on general construction safety programs and courses on specialized areas of the industry. Though they were developed with union funds and for union members, some of Laborers-AGC's films and course materials were used by U.S. and Canadian government agencies for worksite safety and awareness programs. In the mid-1980s, the fund shifted some of its efforts away from construction. Union officials noticed a significant lack of organized workforce development in the burgeoning environmental remediation industry. Labor market projections at that time exposed a potentially severe shortage of skilled environmental remediation workers. In 1987, Laborers-AGC received a grant from the National Institute for Environmental Health Sciences (NIEHS) to develop a program for hazardous waste cleanup workers. Favorable program evaluations led to further grant awards from the Environmental Protection Agency (EPA), U.S. Department of Energy (DOE), U.S. Department of Defense (DOD), and the National Institute for Occupational Safety and Health (NIOSH).

NIEHS and NIOSH distribute grant funds and monitor administrative requirements, but they rely on DOE and DOD for technical standards and evaluation. These agencies are each responsible for particular environmental areas and must regulate all training programs that certify workers for these fields. Because environmental workers handle substances that pose potentially serious risks to public health and safety, they must all be certified to work, and all their training programs must be formally approved to operate. The fund's program specialists, who develop course curricula and train course trainers, must do so in compliance with the mandates of the federal agencies that oversee each work specialization.

In addition to meeting the requirements of the federal agencies, programs often must meet state agency requirements. The differences among the various state and federal standards make it very difficult for Laborers-AGC to achieve programmatic consistency among its environmental courses. Each course (see Table C.1) is

Table C.1

Environmental Remediation Courses

Course	Hours
Hazardous waste operations	45
Hazardous waste worker	80
Asbestos abatement	40
Lead (paint) abatement	40
Radiological worker	32
Underground storage tank removal[a]	32
Confined space entry[a]	32

[a]These are new courses with hands-on activities and written tests but, as of yet, no formal performance assessments.

independent and leads to a specialized certificate, but the fund maintains a single approach for all courses. One standardized element in these courses has been the assessment system used in the environmental remediation courses.

DESCRIPTION AND PURPOSE

The Laborers-AGC Education and Training Fund's environmental training assessment is a flexible system that uses performance-based tests and criterion-referenced multiple-choice tests to measure the competencies and knowledge of environmental trainees. The assessments are designed to certify each individual's competence, as well as to monitor course quality for the purposes of improvement and to report program completion information to the appropriate federal and state agencies. The programs receive federal funding, so the reporting of results is done both to comply with governmental certification requirements and to maintain quality standards and accountability for the ongoing grants or contracts.

The fund developed each assessment tool by employing an assessment expert to work with each course's program specialists and industry experts. In some instances, staff from regulatory agencies were consulted on specific issues. The cost for developing the written and performance assessments was $10,000 to $12,000 for each course, all of it covered by grant funds. Laborers-AGC staff attribute the relatively low development costs to high in-kind contributions from training school instructors and assessment specialists. Also, the fund is just now working to rigorously evaluate the assessments for validity and reliability.

Courses range from thirty-two to eighty hours in length. Students spend roughly half their time in the classroom and half in hands-on field activities; usually they must pass all of the performance tests in order to continue in the course and be eligible to take the multiple-choice exam given on the final day. When they successfully complete both, trainees gain Laborers-AGC–sponsored certification and can work for up to one year in the particular job. To remain eligible for work, they must complete annual refresher courses that update them on new regulations, procedures, and equipment.

Courses have from one to six performance tests, depending on course curriculum and length; each test may assess up to thirty-five tasks. The performance tests last from five to twenty minutes; the simplest requires a trainee to explain his or her actions while testing certain equipment. On the other end of the spectrum, the trainee may perform a complex series of actions in a simulated work procedure. In some courses, performance tests are distinct events that occur separately from the regular training, whereas in others, such tests are used as a training tool and then later as a measurement tool. In the latter case, trainees pair off during the training event, one evaluating the other's performance using a check-off sheet. The instructor monitors the evaluations, with little interference, and uses the same check-off sheet to test the trainees later. This shared evaluation helps trainees build a strong sense of responsibility not only for their own knowledge and performance but also for that of their coworkers, on whom they will rely so heavily at the worksite.

In the hazardous waste worker course, one procedure that is both a training activity and a tested event is decontamination after simulated field work in a Level-A protective suit. Often called a "moon suit," the Level-A fully encapsulates workers and their protective equipment (boots, hard hat, respirator, and air tanks). A trainee enters the three-stage "decon" area wearing the suit and proceeds through a battery of prescribed steps for washing and disrobing. He or she must properly spray and scrub the suit with disinfectant before moving to the disrobing stage, at which point the trainee removes each layer of protective clothing and equipment. Trainees take approximately fifteen minutes to perform all nineteen steps involved in the decon, each of which must be performed properly and in sequence to pass. There is no limit to the number of retests if trainees fail this procedure, since it must be passed to pass the course.

The performance test criteria vary from program to program, according to the degree of oversight by the regulatory agency. For example, the radiological worker course must meet carefully specified DOE regulations. The performance exam for this course thus utilizes importance-weighted point deductions for incorrect performance on tasks. For example, if a trainee fails to remove protective gloves in the proper sequence, two points are deducted, but if he or she improperly responds to an "unusual radiological event," five points are deducted. The underlying factor that determines each task's point weighting is the potential for health and safety risks to the individual, coworkers, or the public if the trainee makes a mistake. Thus, for instance, three of the performance test's twenty-three tasks each carry a possible deduction of twenty-one points—enough to fail the test—because these are crucial tasks that workers must *never* perform improperly. If an individual's point total drops below eighty on the assessment, he or she cannot continue the course. For every task, though, instructors have a box to check if the student recognizes his or her mistake just after making it, notifies the instructor, and rectifies it immediately. The point deductions decrease when trainees correct themselves this way, and, in the case of the three crucial tasks, the decrease is dramatic—from twenty-one points to seven or even three points (see Table C.2). The fund developed these weightings with DOE input and approval.

In contrast, the hazardous waste worker course has no such rigorous level of performance evaluation. The Occupational Safety and Health Administration (OSHA) requires workers in hazardous waste removal to be certified by an approved training provider, but it does not produce regulations that specify what the training must include. Laborers-AGC is left to define the requirements for certification, including designing the performance exam in this case. Each item on the performance exam is simply marked as correct or incorrect. Though it would be possible to generate importance weightings for

Table C.2

Sample Performance Test Items and Scoring from the Radiological Worker Course

	Rating			
	Performs Correctly		Notifies Instructor	
Task	Yes	No	Yes	No
4. Recorded correct information for task on RWP sign-in sheet prior to entry	___	___ −3	___ −2	___ −3
5. Entered only areas identified for tasks on RWP	___	___ −21	___ −7	___ −21
6. Maximized distance, minimized time, and utilized shielding	___	___ −5	___ −3	___ −5

NOTE: RWP = radiological work permit.

each task on this course's exams, Laborers-AGC would have to shoulder the costs of researching them and then justify the weightings to a federal agency that does not even require a performance test.

The written exams are given at the end of each course and consist of either fifty or 100 questions drawn randomly from a large test bank. Laborers-AGC creates the questions for each test and submits them to the appropriate federal agency for approval. The radiation worker course is an exception, though, in that Laborers-AGC staff must randomly select questions from those developed by the DOE. Once tests are formulated, they are disseminated to the training facilities, where local instructors administer them according to program guidelines.

Results of the written exams are tallied for each individual and later aggregated for whole classes, training schools, and the entire training system. Local training schools need student and class results in order to process worker certificates and to comply with state or local regulations for training providers. Laborers-AGC collects all data to monitor both of these functions and to keep track of program performance trends.

The assessment tasks are tied closely to the instructional objectives. These objectives were developed by the fund's content/industry experts and agency staff to mirror the skills needed in the occupation. The hands-on activities contextualize the classroom information in events that will be found at most, if not all, environmental remediation worksites. These field activities use mock hazard sites and actual tools and equipment to ensure that trainees who pass a performance event can work safely and effectively on real worksites.

The knowledge and skills measured by the assessments are highly specific to the occupation and the specialization area. At present, Laborers-AGC is considering ways to combine courses regulated by different agencies so as to create more comprehensive environmental worker courses. Though such courses might have great potential for workers and employers, the fund finds it very difficult to satisfy all the state and federal regulations simultaneously for each individual work area. However, it combines two training courses regulated by OSHA and the DOE (hazardous waste worker and radiological worker, respectively) into a single 120-hour course for workers at nuclear power plants. In January of 1996, program specialists were preparing for a trial run of the course at the Hanford nuclear facility in Washington state. Any significant alterations to these assessments or the curriculum will occur only after a review of course results and input from the agencies. Laborers-AGC administrators are considering how to combine the EPA-regulated asbestos and lead abatement courses into such a "cluster" course, but considerable work with EPA staff will probably be necessary to do so.

Using the fund's curricula is optional for local training schools, but the fact that Laborers-AGC programs have been independently approved by the regulatory agencies definitely makes their use advantageous. Documenting that they use the fund's federally approved program helps schools satisfy most, if not all, of their state's requirements for providers of training in these specializations.

RELATIONSHIP TO OTHER PROGRAMS

Many union laborers consider the environmental training courses useful for career advancement. Many construction laborers seek environmental certifications after working for several years in the construction field (with varying experiences). Union members generally agree that environmental courses are more technical and have more formal testing procedures than most construction courses, thus requiring greater cognitive abilities. The nature of these courses led to development of a preparatory course for union members who want to bolster their basic reading, math, and science skills before enrolling in an environmental course. The preparatory course lasts forty hours, uses some texts and materials from the certification courses, and is usually offered just before many environmental classes start so that the trainees can quickly apply their sharpened skills.

Although the fund's environmental programs are now equal in number and importance to its construction programs, there is little contact between them. They operate under separate departments and, in general, have separate sources of financial support. The construction programs use mainly local training fund contributions, whereas the environmental programs are supported by federal grants. The environmental courses have money to support activities such as hiring consultants to develop assessments and evaluate programs.

The construction programs are less able to do this, but recently the fund's administrators have undertaken an initiative to research and create new performance tests for them. However, until this project is completed, most of the construction programs will continue to use informal instructor observations as the sole means of skill assessment. Environmental and construction programs differ in their level of technicality and certification requirements, and there is less overall consistency among the construction courses. Within the environmental department, though, courses are closely related. Program specialists often cross-train so that they can collaborate on curriculum development and train-the-trainer events. This collaboration helps to increase consistency of training in specialized areas that may be technically dissimilar.

Many other environmental programs also prepare workers for this field, but coordination or cooperation among them is rare and limited. Unions such as the carpenters, teamsters, and operating engineers offer certification programs in the same specializations, as do many private organizations and postsecondary institutions, such as the University of California at Los Angeles. Competition for students is strong. Private training schools and postsecondary institutions compete for students—the former to make profits, the latter to fill enrollment targets. And the unions compete among themselves, each wanting to gain more of the market by placing more of its workers in the courses and then in jobs This latter tension is difficult to resolve because under the NIEHS grant, Laborers-AGC is the primary grant recipient and the teamsters union is a subgrantee. Each is developing independent course curricula, but the fund has additional duties. Laborers-AGC is responsible for all administrative, budgetary, and reporting concerns. Interaction between the two is mainly confined to high-level administrative matters, and staff members do not confer frequently on curricular matters.

Some of the Laborers-AGC courses differ from those offered by other providers in that they require more—sometimes two times more— hours than the regulations mandate. Industry consultants recommended that the fund add time for extensive field exercises and assessment in addition to the time spent on classroom instruction. Not all of these hands-on activities are required by federal agencies, but many have real safety and productivity implications. While the Laborers-AGC hazardous waste worker course is recognized in the industry and agencies for its quality and comprehensiveness, the eighty-hour course time may be a disadvantage. The other unions and the private institutions that offer this worker certification do so in a forty-hour format, which is appealing to those paying for the training: it costs less and responds more quickly to employer requests for qualified workers. Contractors with large cleanup projects do not compare course quality or assessment procedures when trying to meet workforce needs and project deadlines. They simply need certified workers and may call upon another union if it can supply them faster and at lower cost. Because of this pressure, Laborers-AGC is considering designing another version of its field/classroom training in a forty-hour format. Currently, it does not know how this change would affect the assessments.

In addition to the environmental course assessments, trainees in the hazardous waste worker course must successfully pass a physical exam in which a registered nurse tests their pulmonary capacity, heart rate, and blood pressure. The physical exam is given at the outset of the course to provide assurance that each trainee has the physical capacity to perform strenuous training activities (and, later, work) in enclosed suits while wearing respiratory protection. Along with the signed approval of his or her physician, this assessment's results are recorded as part of each person's eligibility for training and subsequent certification. This requirement reduces the legal liability of the fund and the training schools for any incidents that may occur, and screens individuals before they begin the course.

IMPLEMENTATION AND ADMINISTRATION

The traditional model of assessments, multiple-choice final exams, has been used in one or more courses continuously since 1987. As the courses have been developed and come on-line, the assessments have been adapted slightly in order to reflect the standards and certification requirements of each course. Responsibilities for the environmental assessments are divided among staff at Laborers-AGC and staff at the forty training schools that offer at least one environmental course. Program specialists at Laborers-AGC develop and update the tests as well as monitor the quality and consistency of their use at local sites. The fund's director of environmental programs is responsible for overseeing all assessment and other curricular activities.

Training-school staff administer the assessments, score them, and report the results to the fund and to the appropriate state and federal regulatory agencies.

The environmental assessments are updated by the fund once a year, or more frequently if significant changes occur in the industry or its regulations. When considering changes to the assessment, the fund relies on the expertise of its specialists and other industry or regulatory experts, as well as input from course instructors. At its annual instructor development program (IDP), the fund holds educational seminars on professional, technical, and life skills topics for the more than 200 instructors. Also at the IDP, the fund holds curriculum update sessions for each environmental course. In these, instructors can discuss issues directly with specialists, which is a way to maintain course integrity at the local level.

TECHNICAL QUALITY

Laborers-AGC has not extensively evaluated the assessment tools used in its environmental programs. In the late 1980s and early 1990s, much of the fund's efforts concentrated on developing and disseminating courses to meet the training demands of employers and the union. One course after another was developed and brought on-line throughout North America. Staffing and time constraints prevented extensive reliability and validity checks during this period, but the fund has more recently started efforts to evaluate and strengthen the technical quality of its environmental assessments.

Laborers-AGC staff, together with technical and assessment experts, began first by reviewing the oldest assessments—those from the hazardous waste worker course. Though fund staff originally developed the tests for this course with the guidance of similar experts, no experts remained involved throughout the development process, which may have contributed to test weaknesses. After lengthy evaluations of the written test, reviewers found items that did not comply with best-practice guidelines for multiple-choice criterion-referenced exams. The fund set out, with assessment specialists, to remedy the problem items by creating a bank of draft test questions that met the guidelines. These questions were then screened by subject specialists for content validity and by assessment specialists for construct validity. The resulting questions were used in pilot-course trials at several local training schools. Work is currently under way to synthesize the collected feedback from course instructors, students, and program specialists so that final changes can be made to these test items. Once reviewed and corrected, these items will be incorporated into the current test bank, and the same process will be applied to written exams for the other environmental courses.

All the performance exams will eventually undergo comprehensive evaluations, but the fund has not yet determined the process for this. Only the hazardous waste worker course's performance tests have undergone a preliminary evaluation. Content and assessment specialists found that test items are strongly correlated with the work performed on actual worksites, though it is clear to the fund that continual changes in technology, materials, equipment, and practices make content validity an ongoing concern. The items tested in the performance exam were found to closely reflect course content (as reflected in curricular materials), but in some instances they did not closely follow what was actually being taught. For example, certain items in the performance test, as in the written exam, are meant to measure a student's ability to integrate situational facts and circumstances so as to arrive at a proper solution or action. In some course-monitoring visits, reviewers found that instructors were not properly teaching the skills needed to do this. The situational facts were covered, but instructors often did not lead students through the synthesis steps of linking background information and circumstances with possible actions and their likely impacts.

Laborers-AGC considers this flaw both programmatic and instructional and is working to strengthen both the assessment skills of its program specialists (who develop the curricula and train instructors) and the instructional skills of its trainers. Fund staff work with each other and assessment consultants to understand how to develop curricular activities for these skills, and they work with small groups of instructors in yearly instructor refresher sessions to ensure that the skills are taught properly. The work that fund specialists and other staff plus consultants do on curricular and testing updates can be further refined and coordinated at the IDP, where the entire cadre of environmental instructors gathers yearly.

The American Council on Education has also evaluated these environmental courses through its program on noncollegiate-sponsored instruction (PONSI), though to a lesser degree. Instruction and subject experts representing PONSI compared each environmental course's content, learning activities, and assessments with those of current college offerings. Each course was given a recommended number of semester-hour college credits. PONSI reevaluates each course every five years, or sooner if course components are changed. This continuing evaluation is another source of maintaining high quality in the environmental assessment system.

Employers have reacted very positively to the quality of certified employees, which is especially notable because employers are mindful of the potential health and safety ramifications of improperly trained workers. Because the fund is a shared venture between labor and management, employers have immediate input channels if their needs are not being met. The construction and remediation contractors are not the only employers who rely on the assessments to accurately measure skill, though. The DOE, for example, has contracted with the fund to train workers at its headquarters and at several nuclear facilities. DOE experts take great interest in this training because the DOE requires that managers and some engineers at nuclear facilities be certified along with facility technicians. Reaction to the skills assessment from all levels of the DOE and from participating employees has been positive, just as it has from industry contractors and union members. When informal pre- and posttraining comparisons were conducted, workers showed improved knowledge, awareness, and overall performance.

Since the first generation of tests, Laborers-AGC has monitored the exam for any form of gender or racial bias and has made changes when necessary. For the most part, questionable test items are discovered either in monitoring visits or at curriculum update sessions at the IDP each year. Though union membership is roughly half female or minority, assessment results are not aggregated by gender or race/ethnicity to allow such comparisons.

CONSEQUENCES AND USE OF ASSESSMENT RESULTS

An obvious consequence of the assessments is a certificate specifying skill achievement and the attendant acceptance into a specialized field. Moreover, as a result of certification, some trainees have greater confidence in their own skills and knowledge, and they gain greater awareness of the potential effects of their actions on the job. The performance assessments in particular give them the ability to monitor their own work performance and the safety conditions affecting them and their coworkers. At their yearly certification refreshers, many trainees have commented that they mentally "test" their performance while working and, as a result, feel safer and more sure of their decisions in the field.

On the negative side, some potential students who doubt their classroom skills (technical reading, listening for comprehension, etc.) have considerable reservations about enrolling in these courses. Word-of-mouth accounts of the written tests' difficulty particularly cause many to fear that even if they successfully participate in all classroom and hands-on activities, they may fail the final exam. Although the failure rate (on the final exam) for the environmental courses is only about 10 percent, more than half of the students enter courses with a substantial fear of failure, which contributes to a fairly high dropout rate before the exam.

An additional result of the assessments is that some instructors see them as yet another of the fund's curricular mandates. Because local schools are independent, some are reluctant to comply with strict rules or to use required curricular components. Laborers-AGC staff suspect that some assessment rules are not followed from time to time (such as orally translating test questions into other languages), but such deviations are likely isolated and rare. The fund's program specialists visit each school every twelve to eighteen months to monitor particular courses for compliance. If a school blatantly disregards program rules, Laborers-AGC can take sanctions, including withdrawing its sponsorship, in which case the school would have to develop and accredit its own course. This would entail researching technical and pedagogical issues, developing the curriculum and materials, and purchasing new equipment and supplies, in addition to gaining state and federal agencies' approval for the program. This process would be extremely time-consuming and costly, so schools have a strong incentive to comply.

The courses cover a great deal of material, and instructors must essentially teach to the test. This is seen by the fund as both beneficial and necessary, because test-focused instruction gives students an acute sense that all items in the comprehensive course are applicable and important. Laborers-AGC staff see test-focused instruction as contributing to the strong correlation between assessments and work performance and to consistency in instructional and assessment practices across schools.

APPLICABILITY TO VOCATIONAL EDUCATION

The Laborers-AGC assessment model is one that may be applied very easily in vocational education settings. That is, a system of performance-based and written tests is not unusual in vocational settings. But two characteristics of the fund's model would be difficult for many vocational programs to match: the high level of industry support and the high level of funding. A key element of the fund's assessment that would not exist in many vocational settings is the strong systemwide partnership between employers and workers and the input that the employers and workers provide (indeed, gaining substantial input from *either* employers or workers is usually an obstacle). With such regular industry input, Laborers-AGC assessments can test for federally mandated skills as well as those required by employers. The broad industry base that provides this input allows certified workers to gain skill portability and enables training centers to meet many of the common demands local employers voice. Of course, vocational educators may be primarily concerned with the demands of employers in their particular area or state, but as national skill standards are developed, the prospect of a broader, industry-validated assessment may become desirable, and even necessary, in many programs.

Many educators could benefit from an assessment system that can adapt to the different standards and regulations governing occupations. In vocational programs not having a consistent assessment approach among courses, this system could serve as a model for linking common elements and emphasizing them in the courses while still allowing for variation between subjects. Laborers-AGC maintains the work-simulated performance tests and multiple-choice written exam in all courses, even though the nature of the course content and the applicable state and federal regulations may vary considerably.

It is also important to recognize that costs may be a barrier for vocational educators who seek an assessment with the depth and breadth of the hands-on activities in the Laborers-AGC model. Space and equipment requirements for the fund's model are quite high: it is very costly to obtain and prepare areas for practice and performance that closely simulate actual environmental remediation work. The Laborers-AGC assessments rely on intricate and varied field activities to measure how a student will perform on the job. It would not be plausible to conduct the fund's assessments in a small yard or shop bay that must be shared with other classes. Each simulation area is generally dedicated to a narrow range of tasks. For example, the hazardous waste course requires trainees to perform activities in an outdoor field simulating a hazardous substance dump in which they must maneuver to locate and uncover barrels buried in dirt or sunken in small pools of water. Even in the asbestos abatement course, where simulation areas are indoors, the curriculum calls for a dedicated room or properly enclosed structure that allows the simulated asbestos particles to be removed and hauled away, just as would be the case in a true remediation area.

As equally costly as creating the simulated worksites for practice and performance assessments is the use of actual equipment. The courses require enough equipment for all students to use or wear simultaneously. In general, this equipment—respirators, air tanks, and specialized air filtration vacuums—is very costly. Of course, not all vocational courses prepare students for occupations that use expensive tools and equipment, but each prepares them for jobs whose equipment and settings are unique. Without using that equipment in a wider variety of situational applications, as Laborers-AGC does, vocational teachers may not create or maintain such close ties between course content, assessments, and projected job performance.

Once the performance area is established and the equipment purchased, though, the cost of administering the assessments is fairly low. The instructors' time must be paid for (plus a small amount for materials), and more than one instructor must be present for safety and pedagogical reasons if more than five trainees are in certain kinds of protective suits or using certain equipment at one time. The instructors who administer the tests also score them, using criteria or answer sheets provided by Laborers-AGC, so the cost of their labor is the main expense for scoring.

There has been considerable outside interest in Laborers-AGC's environmental programs, though mainly from educators outside the United States. The fund is currently working on implementing some of its curricula with industry training organizations in countries such as Mexico and Russia. Though many environmental problems are common among countries, the new programs and assessments will have to adapt to different government or industry regulations where they exist. Because the assessments developed and used in the United States and Canada were built to accommodate such differences, the fund feels this dissemination effort will progress smoothly. Though generally minor, the adaptations necessary to accommodate differences between U.S. and Canadian regulations will prove valuable as the fund develops these foreign programs.

NATIONAL BOARD FOR PROFESSIONAL TEACHING STANDARDS CERTIFICATION PROGRAM

The National Board for Professional Teaching Standards (NBPTS) was established to develop and administer a voluntary system of advanced professional certification to recognize highly accomplished K–12 teachers. The standards guiding task development were developed by committees of teachers and scholars. To obtain the NBPTS certificate, teachers prepare an extensive portfolio demonstrating their preparation, classroom work, teaching strategies, instructional goals and results, students' work, and professional activities. In addition, they participate in one day of performance activities at a regional assessment center. The process takes up to one school year to complete.

NBPTS certification offers benefits to teachers, school districts, and teacher training institutions. Teachers have an opportunity to reflect on and perhaps improve their teaching skills and professional life. School districts have an independent standard against which to measure the ability of their experienced teachers, and the process clarifies for teacher training institutions what accomplished teachers should know and be able to do. Ultimately, the most important beneficiaries of improved teaching practices are students.

DESCRIPTION AND PURPOSE

NBPTS, a nonprofit organization, was founded and initially funded by the Carnegie Corporation of New York to provide avenues for teachers to demonstrate their professional achievement. Establishment of NBPTS in 1987 fulfilled a major recommendation of *A Nation Prepared: Teachers for the 21st Century,* a report issued by the

Carnegie Task Force on Teaching as a Profession (1986). NBPTS hopes to improve the public's perception of teachers, enhance teachers' own view of their profession, and thereby attract and retain high-quality teachers.

A majority of the sixty-three NBPTS members are classroom teachers actively engaged in instruction, and many others are teacher educators or leaders of teacher professional associations. Other members include public officials, board of education members, administrators, presidents and faculty of higher education institutions, parents, minority student rights advocates, and business leaders. A majority of the public and other educator members are elected or appointed public officials. Reaching consensus on the standards among such a broad stakeholder group has been a long process, as has developing, testing, and administering assessment tasks. To date, these activities have cost tens of millions of dollars. Although NBTPS planned on high costs, especially for developing and testing initial assessments, it aims to make development and administration of the remaining assessments more efficient and economical.

NBPTS has a threefold mission: "To establish high and rigorous standards for what teachers should know and be able to do, to certify teachers who meet those standards, and to advance other education reforms for the purpose of improving student learning in American schools" (NBPTS, 1989, p. 1). Its core activity is an assessment system organized around subjects and age levels. NBPTS will combine four age groupings and fourteen subjects to produce its range of certificates (see Table D.1), which will total thirty or more (some subjects cover two age groups combined). In 1995–1996, NBPTS certification was available in two categories: early childhood/generalist (EC/G) and middle childhood/generalist (MC/G).

RELATIONSHIP TO OTHER PROGRAMS

NBPTS certification complements but does not replace state licensing. State licensing systems set compulsory minimum standards for novice teachers; NBPTS certification creates voluntary standards for accomplished teachers. Similarly, NBPTS standards should build upon but not substitute for requirements for preservice training.

Table D.1

Current and Planned NBPTS Certificates

Levels	Subject Areas
Early childhood (ages 3–8), middle childhood (ages 7–12), and early adolescence (ages 11–15)	Generalist
Middle childhood (ages 7–12), early adolescence (ages 11–15), and adolescence and young adulthood (ages 14–18+)	English language arts, mathematics, science, social studies/history
Early–middle childhood (ages 3–12), and early adolescence–young adulthood (ages 11–18+)	Foreign language, art, music, exceptional needs/generalist, English as a new language, physical education, library/media, guidance counseling
Early adolescence–young adulthood (ages 11–18+)	Health, vocational education

Teacher training institutions develop curriculum to comply with state laws; NBPTS standards establish a set of profession-endorsed guidelines for best practices that schools can use in improving in-service training (e.g., when developing curriculum to organize the continuing education of teachers).

The teaching profession is attempting to link accreditation, licensure, and advance certification with the goal of ensuring that all students are taught by competent, professional teachers (Rahn, 1995). Two national organizations (the National Council for Accreditation of Teacher Education [NCATE] and the Interstate New Teacher Assessment and Support Consortium [INTASC], a project of the Council of Chief State School Officers), the two teacher unions (the National Education Association and the American Federation of Teachers), and others are working with NBPTS to improve the profession of teaching for both teachers and students. They envision a linked system of preservice preparation, extended clinical training, and continuing professional development in which National Board certification plays an important role. Although much of this linkage is still under development, both NCATE and INTASC are taking steps to see that their own components of this process are aligned with the work of NBPTS. Similarly, input from relevant professional committees and other stakeholders is actively sought in every phase of implementing the NBPTS system—from the composition of the board of directors, standards committees, and field test network that operated from 1993 to 1995, to the broad-based review of documents and test packages.

IMPLEMENTATION AND ADMINISTRATION

Implementation of the teacher assessment system builds on a strong base of educational research and broad support among established educational organizations and stakeholders. The first task of NBPTS was "to identify the knowledge, skills, and dispositions that describe accomplished teaching and to convert those attributes into high and rigorous standards upon which to base the National Board Certification system" (NBPTS, Executive Committee, 1989, p. 2). NBPTS staff reviewed the relevant literature on these issues and the standard-setting work of other occupations and obtained comments from leaders in the education community before issuing *Toward High and Rigorous Standards for the Teaching Profession* (NBPTS, 1989).

This 1989 document established the philosophical underpinnings for the program, including the prerequisites for applying (three years of teaching and, at a minimum, a baccalaureate degree); five propositions that set forth broad principles to guide the development of standards; and assessment activity development guidelines. NBPTS established a comprehensive organizational structure and process to develop the assessment system, with teachers playing a major role in almost every area.

Through a national competitive process, contractors were selected for several development and implementation tasks. Assessment development laboratories (ADLs) developed and tested the assessment tasks. A field test network (FTN) was engaged in the early years to provide candidates, administrators, scorers, and evaluations of the methods and systems. The operation of the system was assigned to another contractor. A technical analysis group (TAG) provided research support to the other contractors (e.g., a literature review of assessment methods in other professions; development of the sampling frame of teachers for the field-test trials) and analysis of the work of the standards committees, ADLs, and other contractors. In the past year, most of these functions have been consolidated in the hands of a single contractor, Educational Testing Service.

The development process was implemented gradually. Initially, two standards committees were appointed; then additional committees were added each year. Once the initial standards committees began work, an ADL was appointed to work with each of the committees. A year and a half later, a request for proposal (RFP) for six additional ADLs was issued. This strategy of gradual growth allowed NBPTS to learn from early experiences and adjust the process.

Because the process of establishing the assessment system may provide a useful model for establishing a system for recognizing accomplished vocational teachers, it is described in considerable detail here. A vocational education standards committee has been appointed and has issued a set of draft standards that have now been through the NBPTS public comment and critique process.

Developing Standards

Standards committees are composed primarily of teachers but also include researchers and others involved in the field of interest. The first four committees were appointed in 1990 for early adolescence/ English language arts (EA/ELA), early adolescence/generalist (EA/G), adolescence and young adulthood/mathematics, and early adolescence through young adulthood/art. By 1995, seventeen committees had been established to set standards in twenty-one of the more than thirty certification fields (Bradley, 1995a); by 1997, initial development had been completed and standards were released for public comment in these twenty-one areas.

Committee members are selected through a process that gathers nominations from a broad group of professional organizations, NBPTS members, and NBPTS staff. For the EA/G committee, for example, over 130 nominations were reviewed to find thirteen members who provided a balance of gender, location, and profession (Hattie, Sackett, and Millman, 1994). Members of the relevant ADL participate in standards committee meetings. Key professional organizations are also invited to appoint liaisons who attend all committee meetings, e.g., the International Reading Association provided a liaison to the EA/G committee.

These committees develop draft standards for the knowledge and skills that teachers should have to achieve NBPTS certification. Draft standards are reviewed by NBPTS, its certification standards working group (CSWG), field site members, the ADL, and a broad spectrum of stakeholders. Reviewers were asked to rate the standards for clarity and for their relevance to highly accomplished teaching, among other factors. One issue that arose in the review of the initial EA/G standards was the difficulty of determining appropriate subject matter for generalist teachers. The standards committee makes recommendations to the board, which has final authority in making decisions. Almost thirty months after their first meeting, NBPTS and its CSWG approved the standards for the 1993–1994 EA/G field test. Revised standards were approved the following year for the 1994–1995 administration. While standard setting proved to be a lengthy process, a survey of the reviewers indicated widespread approval for the standards' validity among both teachers and nonteachers.[1]

Assessment Development Laboratories

ADLs worked with one or more standards committees to develop and produce an assessment package. ADLs were selected through a competitive merit review RFP process (NBPTS, 1990a and 1990b). Guidelines for the ADLs stated that all assessments had to be professionally credible, publicly acceptable, legally defensible, administratively feasible, and economically affordable. Potential contractors were directed to include multiple forms of assessment and to consider how student learning as a measure of teacher effectiveness might be demonstrated.

The following six assessment methods were specified for exploration: (1) a portfolio of classroom teaching accomplishments that includes evidence of the teacher's participation in a learning community, samples of student work, and artifacts produced by the teacher; (2) observations of the teacher in his or her classroom; (3) structured interviews based in part on the portfolio; (4) exercises typical of the

---

[1]About 87 percent of teachers and 88 percent of nonteachers responded "agree" or "strongly agree" that "each of the 11 standards describes a critical aspect of highly accomplished teaching practice within this field" (Hattie, Sackett, and Millman, 1994, p. 34).

teacher's work, e.g., viewing videotape of a teaching situation and grading samples of students' work resulting from that situation; (5) simulations that are "contextual assessments," e.g., suggesting more effective strategies after viewing a videotape of the teacher's performance; and (6) written tests of subject matter knowledge and pedagogy. The following components were also to be included in the assessment procedures: (1) documentation of the teacher's practice and thinking through videotapes, student work, other artifacts, and commentaries; and (2) assessment of the candidate's subject matter knowledge, knowledge of pedagogy, and knowledge of child development for the specific age group.

The first ADL contract was awarded in 1990 to the University of Pittsburgh School of Education and the Connecticut Department of Education to develop assessments for the EA/ELA certificate. The second contract was awarded to the Performance Assessment Laboratory at the University of Georgia for the EA/G certificate.

Both labs devised roughly similar assessment activities that could be closely integrated with class lessons, such as developing appropriate applications for a new classroom resource, recording actual classroom plans and activities and analyzing what occurred, or analyzing and evaluating samples of student writing. Emphasis in the assessments is on giving teachers an opportunity to show what they know in an authentic context, rather than on pinpointing what they do not know. For both certificates, teachers complete activities at the school site, collecting documentation in a portfolio, and perform additional activities at the testing center. Tables D.2 and D.3 compare the skills and activities targeted by each lab at, respectively, the school site and the assessment center (Bradley, 1994).

The first field test, which functioned like a real assessment, revealed strengths and weaknesses in the assessment center model. More than one-third (eighty-one out of 289) EA/G candidates participating in the 1993–1994 field test were certified (the certificates were awarded in January 1995). Successful EA/ELA candidates were certified that summer. The two certificates were offered again in 1994–1995 to fee-paying candidates, and about 200 candidates participated. At a minimum, fourteen assessors were required to score each candidate's work (two scores for each of seven exercises) during this first year. Problems with the scoring procedures resulted in a

Table D.2

School Site Skills and Activities Targeted by Each Lab

Early Adolescence/Generalist	Early Adolescence/English Language Arts
1. Professional development and service: submit vita; write accounts of 1) an impact of professional development on practice and 2) professional service activity; obtain letters of support from colleagues.	1. Professional background: submit resume; write one- to two-page description of participation in a learning community.
2. Teaching and learning: write narrative describing a selected class over a period of time; describe the progress of three students, reflecting different learning characteristics; videotape class activities; provide samples of student work and teaching practices.	2. Teaching and learning: describe and analyze the writing of three students, including the influence of instruction (submit with five to eight samples of the students' writing).
3. Lesson analysis: select unedited 30–45 minute videotape from a class and write account of the teaching and learning that occurred, highlighting five to seven particularly important points.	3. Interpretive discussion: videotape 15 to 20 minutes of a class discussing a piece of literature; write an evaluation of the discussion.
	4. Planning and teaching: write eight-page commentary describing planning and instruction over a three-week period, using an integrated curriculum that demonstrates cultural awareness; include videotape of one class session.

costly redesign of the scoring system and delays in announcing the results (Bradley, 1995a). This particular certification was revised and then offered again in 1996–1997. Reducing the complexity of the scoring process was critical. Modifications focused on making the assessments less burdensome to scorers and candidates. According to James R. Smith, NBPTS senior vice president, the initial portfolios, for example, asked for more material than was necessary and needed to be more focused (Bradley, 1995a).

Table D.3

Assessment Center Skills and Activities Targeted by Each Lab

Early Adolescence/Generalist	Early Adolescence/English Language Arts
1. Instructional resources: write analysis of the potential of SimCity for teaching social studies, math, history, and science. (SimCity is a computer simulation supplied to the candidate at the school site.)	1. Group discussion: with other candidates, develop a curriculum unit on personal relationships. Unit materials are selected from eight novels provided previously at school site. Discussion is videotaped.
2. Instructional analysis: write analysis of videotape and materials from a mathematics instructor, including suggestions for more effective strategies and extension of the topic to the arts.	2. Instructional analysis: analyze videotape of teacher-led discussion, including suggestions for improving instruction; show knowledge of young adolescent learning, and demonstrate cultural awareness and understanding of discussion dynamics.
3. Curriculum issues: after group discussion of a theme related to exploration of governmental systems, ecosystems, and the media, complete two-hour written description of the instructional development of a theme drawing on one of the above subjects.	3. Analysis of student writing: analyze set of student papers and discuss analysis with interviewer, making suggestions for improving students' writing. Videotaped.
4. Content knowledge: three one-hour written subject examinations.	4. Content knowledge: three two-hour essay assessments on composition, literature, and language. Literature and journal articles are used for the essay prompts.

Assessment Administration

The first field tests indicated that candidates felt they did not have enough time to prepare their portfolios, but once NBPTS moved to regular operation, the time allowed for portfolio development was lengthened. The 100 hours teachers spent assembling their portfolios was about twice the time NBPTS had anticipated (Bradley, 1994).

Findings from the first set of assessments (Scriven, 1994) point to several problems. Many candidates said that they were influenced to participate by the absence of a fee, so the cost of the actual examination may discourage some potential candidates. (Since the field test, many states and districts have agreed to pay the cost for teachers who choose to apply, so economic factors will not be that much of a deterrent.) The description of the process needs to be clearer so that candidates know what to expect about the amount of time involved and the content of the exercises. About half of the candidates found the instructions for the portfolio exercises unsatisfactory, and most candidates felt the support provided was inadequate. Teachers sought more specific direction for activities, including, for example, the expected length for written assignments.[2] Peer support groups were judged very successful in helping to prepare materials; however, the help of principals was not useful. About half of the participants found preparation workshops and video support useful.

At the testing center, about 75 percent of the candidates bemoaned the lack of computers for the writing tasks. (NBPTS has since chosen Sylvan Technology Centers as the sites for performance activities, so computers are now available.) The amount of writing required was also thought to be excessive. Observers also indicated that testing coordinators needed to be better trained. The original twelve-hour day was problematic; it was subsequently reduced to eight hours. A particularly troubling finding was that about 40 percent of participants felt that seeking certification placed them at some risk in their schools. Michael Scriven, the evaluator of the test administration, noted that this was "consistent with other evidence that teachers tend to identify efforts to excel as egotistical or undemocratic" (Scriven, 1994, p. 9) . He warned that if merit pay was tied to certification, it could increase negative reactions, particularly if principals share this attitude.

Based on the experiences of the first two labs, the draft RFP for subsequent ADLs outlined a streamlined process that would save time and money (NBPTS, 1991). It also addressed many of the concerns raised by Scriven.

---

[2]Bradley (1994) notes that of three Fairfax County, VA, candidates for the EA/G, one's teaching and learning commentary was sixty-six pages, another's was six pages, and the third's was one page.

Field Test Network

Once the labs developed tasks, they were field tested (during 1993–1995) through a national FTN of more than 100 school districts. The network included 165,000 teachers, 25 percent of whom were members of a minority group. Districts in the network have a two-year contract to perform a variety of tasks, including reviewing standards, developing staff development programs for candidates, and field testing assessment packages (NBPTS, 1992). The sites participate on an as-needed basis as the examinations are developed. For example, twenty-six sites participated in the first field test.

Scoring Assessments

Scorers are recruited regionally and receive training on the goals of NBPTS, the standards for each certificate, and the scoring guidelines for each activity. During the field tests, exercises were scored independently by two teachers with training in the appropriate subject, teaching experience, and a recommendation for teaching quality (criteria similar to those demanded of candidates). NBPTS is gradually increasing the proportion of scorers for each certificate who are NBPTS-certified teachers from that field, and eventually all will be. If there are differences in the scores, the scorers meet and discuss the evidence, then independently rescore the exercise. If differences still exist, a third scorer is brought in. The final score represents agreement between two of the three scores (NBPTS, 1995).

Overall Progress

Considerable progress has been made toward NBPTS's long-term goals for increasing the professionalization of teaching. NBPTS has undertaken key steps for developing the certification system and completed many of them. For example, draft standards in twenty-one of the thirty-plus areas have been released for public comment. Yet progress in implementing the assessments has been slowed by the need to revise scoring methods to maintain the board's high standards for quality. Certification was offered in only two areas in

1994–1995, and six certificates, instead of the projected nine, will be available in 1996–1997:

- Early adolescence/generalist
- Early adolescence/English language arts
- Early childhood/generalist
- Middle childhood/generalist
- Adolescence and young adulthood/mathematics
- Early adolescence through young adulthood/art

NBPTS responded to problems and criticisms that arose in early testing. As a result, both the time required for development and the cost of administration have been greater than anticipated. NBPTS has received over $50 million since its inception in October 1987— $37 million from private donors and foundations, and $19.34 million in one-to-one matching funds from the federal government (Bradley, 1995a)—but this has not been enough to maintain the initial development schedule. In 1995, overall cost overruns caused the organization to cancel three of the seven ADL contracts.

Administering the evaluation to the first group of candidates cost more than $4,000 per teacher (not counting development costs). Bradley (1995a) reported that "most of the expenses . . . went to scoring each candidate's work, an exhaustive process that in some cases took 23 hours." Costs for administering the second round of EA/G and EA/ELA tests (1995–1996) were reduced to $3,000 per participant. And costs for the field tests of the early childhood/generalist and middle childhood/generalist certificates were projected to be about $2,500 per participant (Bradley, 1995a). The application fee for the first post-field-test year was $975, but was raised to $2,000 for 1996–1997 and 1997–1998.

The desire to produce innovative assessments (using authentic measures wherever possible) while maintaining very high standards for technical quality has contributed to high costs. NBPTS has implemented many suggestions for reducing costs—e.g., limiting assessments at the testing center to one day instead of two. Consideration is being given to a multiphase process that may also reduce scoring costs and could allow for partial credit (banking of accomplishments). Despite the substantial time burden (reduced from the first field test) on candidates, those who complete the process generally find it to be extremely rewarding.

TECHNICAL QUALITY

Since it began to develop its certification system, NBPTS has been concerned about producing a high-quality and technically defensible process. After the first round of certifications, NBPTS convened a panel of respected educational researchers to review the development of the certification system and determine whether the process was sound from a technical standpoint. The panel concluded that there were "no technical impediments to the Board's use of its Early Adolescence/Generalist assessment to award National Board Certification to candidates whose performances satisfy the ... final recommended performance standard" (Bond et al., 1994, p. 33).

However, the expert panel also recommended that further study be directed as follows:

- To increasing the reliability of the assessment (to resolve problems about scores near the passing standard).

- To determining whether having two content standards assessed less frequently than the others is acceptable.

- To exploring strategies to reduce possible adverse impacts, i.e., the likelihood that the percentage of African American candidates who would be certified would be far lower than that of non-Hispanic white candidates.

- To developing additional forms of the assessment center exercises.

Subsequently, the TAG offered guidance to the assessment developers and evaluated the quality of the certification procedures. During its first year, the TAG either conducted or commissioned eight studies of the technical quality of the 1993–1994 EA/G assessment (Hattie, Sackett, and Millman, 1994; Lloyd and Crocker, no date; Scriven, 1994; Felker, 1994; Heider et al., 1994; Traub, 1994a,b; Jaeger, 1994; Bond and Linn, 1994). The topics of these studies were

1. The development process for content standards

2. Content validity

3. Quality of field-test operations

4. Quality of assessors' training

5. Validity of the application of scoring procedures

6. Consistency of certification decisions and reliability of exercises

7. Recommended performance standards

8. Adverse impacts of differing certification rates of diverse groups

CONSEQUENCES AND USE OF ASSESSMENT RESULTS

Assessment developers learned several lessons from the scoring exercises and from debriefing participants (Bradley, 1995b). Scoring of the first set of portfolios indicated that teachers were not skilled at reflecting on their own work; they were also more comfortable describing rather than analyzing teaching practices. In response, NBPTS developed better instructions for each exercise and clearer guidelines for teachers in order to emphasize analysis as well as description. Moreover, interviewing teachers at the assessment center about the work in their portfolios was also problematic. Identifying and training skilled interviewers is difficult and costly, and this proved not to be the most cost-effective assessment method. Classroom videotapes and samples of student work proved to be more reliable measures of teacher practices than teachers' own descriptions.

While point-in-time samples of student work provided little information about how student learning progressed, they could provide worthwhile information about the quality of the specific assignments. Developers also improved test validity over time by linking testing activities more closely to the skill they wanted to evaluate, e.g., a videotaped student presentation of a class project does not help assessors evaluate the teacher.

Formal support for teachers who apply and rewards for those who are certified are gradually growing in states and districts. Merit pay ("pay for knowledge"), mentor status, the right to teach in any state, and waiver of credential renewal requirements are all rewards that school districts or states can consider. About thirty states have implemented some type of recognition, incentive, or support. North Carolina financially supports teachers who are pursuing the certificate and rewards teachers who obtain it. North Carolina provides the assessment fee, several days' preparation time, and a 4 percent salary increase for teachers who obtain NBPTS certification (Hunt, 1995). North Carolina, Iowa, New Mexico, and Oklahoma waive state licensing requirements for NBPTS-certified teachers who move to the state. Massachusetts and Ohio accept the NBPTS certificate in lieu of their own state recertification (Richardson, 1995).

NBPTS intends for the assessment process itself to give teachers an opportunity to grow professionally by reflecting on their skills and knowledge, and to measure themselves against objective, peer-developed standards (NBPTS, 1995). This focus in the test on content-specific pedagogy forces teachers to carefully examine this central aspect of practice. Test developers also hope that exposure to new techniques and materials will provide teachers with professional growth opportunities, such as might be gained by exploring the relevance of a computer simulation to their instructional strategies (Cape, Dickey, and Anderson, 1995). For example, an EA/G candidate found that "examining his own professional development was a worthwhile activity that helped him clarify who he is as a teacher. Exploring ways to integrate other subjects into his lessons was particularly exciting" (Bradley, 1994).

APPLICABILITY TO VOCATIONAL EDUCATION

The NBPTS experience offers three kinds of lessons for vocational educators. First, the NBPTS experience shows how difficult it can be to use alternative assessments when high stakes are tied to the results. Candidates expect that NBPTS certification will be accompanied by professional recognition and even financial rewards. NBPTS intends for the certification process and standards to drive preservice and inservice training and affect state licensing standards. Consequently, it adopted an approach to insure that the profession endorsed the standards and that the certification process met the highest criteria for quality and fairness. To produce the standards, NBPTS included multiple stakeholders in frequent reviews and instituted systematic quality control procedures. Its commitments to use alternative assessment strategies and to maintain high standards for reliability and validity have made the process complex and necessitated additional professional review and analysis. All this translates into time and expense.

The experience of the ADLs presents a useful picture of the complexity associated with alternative assessments. Following NBPTS's lead, the ADLs tried to be innovative and rely on authentic assessments to measure teacher competence. They developed interesting, relevant, and meaningful exercises for teachers, but in some cases, the activities did not necessarily reflect the underlying competencies they were designed to measure; in other cases, it was difficult for raters to agree on the quality of a candidate's performance. Because ADLs were using new assessment methods, they often could not rely on traditional approaches to monitor quality and thus had to develop new approaches. In fact, NBPTS employed a TAG to consult with and review the work of the ADLs because the test developers were breaking new ground. To its credit, NBPTS set high standards for itself, monitored the assessments carefully, and invested the resources and the time necessary to correct problems. This experience provides a sense of the level of complexity that may be encountered if alternative assessments are used in high-stakes contexts.

These issues should not be unfamiliar to vocational educators, particularly those in the health professions. Requirements for professional credibility and legal defensibility have led to very thorough and comprehensive assessment efforts in the health fields. However, in most cases these professional assessments use traditional techniques, such as multiple-choice and short-answer questions. It is the combination of high-stakes certification and alternative assessments that creates challenges for both quality and defensibility. Vocational educators have used alternative assessments at the classroom level for years, because they link classroom and work experience more closely. The concerns raised here should not weigh too heavily on teachers who want to use more authentic assessments as part of their program. However, quality issues demand greater attention if the assessments become part of a certification system that has important rewards for students.

The second lesson that can be drawn from the NBPTS experience relates to evaluating vocational educators. NBPTS intends to offer a single certification in vocational education (early adolescence through young adulthood). However, it encountered some difficulty in developing the standards because of disagreement about whether general standards could be used for all vocational educators or each occupational area had to be treated separately. In the end, the standards development committee agreed on a single standards framework that recognizes eight distinct areas of industry-specific knowledge: agriculture and environmental sciences; arts and communication; business, marketing, and information management; consumer sciences; health services; human services; manufacturing and engineering technology; and technology education.   The framework also says that there is a common core of vocational knowledge appropriate to all fields—understanding workplace basic skills, commanding general industrial knowledge, and integrating vocational content with core disciplines—as well as industry-specific knowledge. The framework is now available in draft form for public comment. The discussion of what general standards covering vocational education should look like is likely to increase in importance as education moves toward greater integration of vocational and academic curricula and as emphasis shifts in vocational programs from specific occupational skills to broader aspects of an industry.

The third lesson from the NBPTS experience focuses on the value of using assessments to encourage teachers to reflect on and improve their practices and to collaborate with their peers. NBPTS has initiated a process in which teachers put together portfolios to demonstrate aspects of their work, analyze and think about ways to improve their practices, and discuss and critique the work of peers in support groups designed to elicit all candidates' best efforts. This process shows promise for changing the historic isolation most teachers face in their work and for enriching professional development, with the ultimate goal of improving instruction.

OKLAHOMA DEPARTMENT OF VOCATIONAL-TECHNICAL EDUCATION COMPETENCY-BASED TESTING PROGRAM

DESCRIPTION AND PURPOSE

The Oklahoma competency-based testing program encompasses a range of criterion-referenced multiple-choice assessments and performance-based assessments that test the competency attainment of students in both comprehensive high school vocational programs and vocational technical centers. The Oklahoma Department of Vocational-Technical Education (Oklahoma Vo-Tech), a separate agency from the Oklahoma Department of Education, developed and oversees these tests. The testing system as a whole is used to achieve two objectives:

- Program improvement and accountability at the state level (providing data for the occupational competency attainment measure in the state's Perkins performance measures and standards).

- Improvement in instruction and student learning through competency-based curriculum and assessment.

In addition, in some occupational areas, testing has a third purpose: certifying that students have attained competencies for employment purposes.

Written, criterion-referenced multiple-choice tests have been developed for 250 occupational titles that are categorized into approximately fifty-five program areas. A new written test is administered every year for each of the job titles. Advisory groups have been established for each of the program areas to create duty/task lists and to rank tasks by importance (based on how frequently they come up on the job). Questions are written using these lists and are stored in a secure test bank. State staff randomly select test items to develop the annual written tests, which require a minimum score of 70 percent for passing. Oklahoma Vo-Tech is no longer creating assessments in areas involving licensure procedures, such as aircraft maintenance and cosmetology. However, the Oklahoma Department of Health has contracted with Oklahoma Vo-Tech to develop and administer their licensure exams (this aspect is discussed further in a later section).

Students are required to pass performance assessments before they are allowed to take the written test. Though instructors must use the statewide written test, they are free to select tasks for the performance assessment from state-developed ones or other sources, or to use their own performance assessments. Students are asked to show their competence in all the duty areas for a given occupation. Instructors are not required to report passing rates for performance assessments or to provide evidence that students passed the tests to the state, only to keep documentation at the school site for state review and audit purposes.

Performance assessments may be administered throughout the year or at a single point in time. Written assessments are administered at various times during the school year on dates set by the school. After taking the written test on the selected day, students may retake it as many times as the instructor and school allow.

Results on written assessments are reported to the individual students and instructors. Testing liaisons/assessment coordinators at the school site receive a report that describes the performance of the program as a whole in each duty area. Scores are not used to compare different programs; they are aggregated only to compare programs to a standard. In fact, neither superintendents, principals, the state director, nor the assistant director can access individual or program aggregate scores, because the department fears they could misinterpret the data. Only the state-level program manager and his or her staff can access the data.

Curriculum guides that closely follow the task lists have been developed for most occupational titles. Most schools use the curriculum guides, but doing so is optional. Curriculum guides include a posttest, which in practice is now used as both pretest and posttest in order to measure competency gains. These are reported by the testing liaison for the gain measure included in the 1990 Perkins Act–mandated performance measures and standards. Scores from the written assessments are used for the attainment measure.

IMPLEMENTATION AND ADMINISTRATION

The assessment system has been fully operational for the last ten years. Advisory committees continue to meet annually to revise task lists and tests. Before new tests are administered every year, each advisory committee reviews the items on its test. The committee for each occupation includes representatives from labor, higher education, secondary faculty, and industry.

Three test specialists (state-level Vo-Tech staff) are in charge of the fifty-five program areas. Each of these specialists thus coordinates the advisory committee's work, test development, administration, and scoring. It is very difficult for staff to keep the task lists up to current standards given this heavy workload. Task lists are thoroughly reviewed every three years.

State staff rely on testing liaisons at each school site to administer the written tests. Testing liaisons must be trained in the areas of objectivity, test security, and administration. Testing liaisons in all five regions received extensive training in 1993 and now receive updates every August at the annual vocational conference. In addition, staff work with the educators who train student teachers, so student teachers are familiar with the curriculum guides and tests before they become teachers. The liaisons were also given inservice training on performance assessment, but the state has no intention of centralizing that procedure.

Machine-readable forms used for the written competency tests are mailed to the testing division throughout the year. Individual and group results are reported at the end of May for each program, along with the mean percentage correct statewide. These scores are used by individual teachers for measuring classroom performance, and by the testing liaison to report competency attainment for program areas for the statewide measures and standards. Competency gain is reported from scores on the pre- and posttest included in the curriculum guides. Unlike the written tests, the hands-on component is not secured, nor is it administered consistently.

RELATIONSHIP TO OTHER PROGRAMS

For the past eight years, the state agency has provided the Vocational-Technical Education Consortium of States (V-TECS) with duty task lists and tests, but it does not give V-TECS access to the test bank. The state wants the test bank to remain secure. Oklahoma Vo-Tech's assessment system also coordinates the assessments administered statewide by the health certification project and AGC programs (discussed in later sections).

TECHNICAL QUALITY

Based on some pilot testing, the state staff and committees believe that scores on the multiple-choice test are closely linked to job performance. Because they believe there is no real need for a statewide evaluation of the performance assessment system (and because of the high cost of conducting one), they have opted not to pursue such an evaluation. The staff make reference to military research showing that cognitive knowledge (tested in multiple-choice format) is the best indicator of performance (knowledge transfer). No formal study has been conducted to investigate correlations between the performance components and written tests. The state office does not collect data on the failure rates on performance tests conducted at local sites.

State staff conduct item analyses on each multiple-choice test question to look for questions that are too difficult or that show gender or racial/ethnic bias. If they find test items that students are consistently not getting right, they review the items carefully and possibly throw them out. Staff also look at the number of tests administered to each student and the number (and percentage) of students retesting.

State staff feel confident in their tests' content validity because of the employer input to the assessment system. The committees meet regularly to update task lists and test questions in order to ensure that the system continues to be useful in opening up employment opportunities for students.

CONSEQUENCES AND USE OF ASSESSMENT RESULTS

The assessment system has always been implemented on a partly voluntary basis. Local sites are directed to use the system by Oklahoma's state staff, which has more centralized control than most states (for fiscal and historical reasons). However, there are no real consequences for not using the state-prescribed system, and the twenty-nine districts (fifty-nine campuses) can choose which measures and standards to comply with. Under the system of performance measures and standards required by Perkins, school use of the competency-based assessment system has dramatically increased. Local programs receiving federal funds are required to report their performance using these written assessment results.

However, because of this connection with Perkins, instructors more often than not view the tests as contributing to the state agency's accountability system, rather than as a system developed for certifying students or for program improvement. At this point, many instructors use the tests mainly to comply with the state system. Some instructors have difficulty seeing the connection between what they teach in class and what is tested on the competency assessments. One reason for this lack of connection is that the curriculum guide (which teaches to the test) is used inconsistently across schools and occupational areas. Many instructors, schools, and districts use their own texts and other curriculum components instead.

The state recently implemented a "career passport" (i.e., a career-focused portfolio) system. It contains rich information on individual student skills that can be shown to potential employers. There are six required components: evidence of a high school diploma (or GED), vocational program completion, competency in one or more vocational areas (demonstrated by passing approved tests), completion of minimum academic course requirements, adequate attendance, and a resume. State staff hope that students and instructors will see the value of earning a passport and therefore begin to see the competency-based tests as part of a certification process, rather than solely as a way to meet accountability requirements. Participation in the passport system is also voluntary.

APPLICABILITY TO VOCATIONAL EDUCATION

Oklahoma has a strong tradition of vocational education, including centralized state control and substantial state funding, which contributes to the successful operation of the assessment system. States lacking a strong funding base and a centralized system of vocational education may be hard-pressed to follow Oklahoma's example. Oklahoma has both vocational-technical centers (fifty-nine campuses) and comprehensive high schools in twenty-nine districts. Each is governed and funded by a separate structure. Through the state board of vocational-technical education, the state budget funds six of the fifteen staff in the testing division. Testing liaisons at each center are essential to the system. Most of the funding for the liaisons and for other costs of operating local test centers comes from local government sources; however, about 20 percent of the testing liaison's job is dedicated to the state's assessment system.

Oklahoma also points to the difficulty of implementing a state-driven, centralized assessment system that is perceived as relevant at the local level. Many instructors find that the state tests and their course curriculum differ in scope. For example, an instructor of advanced electronics focuses on microcomputer skills and knowledge, but his or her students must take the "general technician" test, which is much broader in scope. In contrast, a business/technology instructor in a systems management program teaches general computer skills, not job-specific skills such as "receptionist/word processor." In this case, the test content may be somewhat narrower than the curriculum.

OKLAHOMA HEALTH CERTIFICATION

Description and Purpose

The Health Certification Project is administered jointly by Oklahoma Vo-Tech and the Oklahoma Department of Health. Certification is currently administered in six areas: long-term care nurse aide, home health care aide, medication aide, adult day care nurse aide, developmentally disabled nurse aide, and residential care nurse aide. Students complete a training program that is approved by the Oklahoma Department of Health and then take a two-part test:

- A clinical skills test in which candidates perform tasks related to client care.

- A written test of seventy to ninety multiple-choice questions.

About 10,000 students complete the assessments each year in the six areas currently in operation. An RN or LVN must approve the clinical performance part of the test, which covers three selected objectives that change from year to year (these are selected from a comprehensive list of objectives). The testing liaison trains the RN or LVN to be a test judge, using a guide developed by the state. Only forty-three test sites may administer the written portion of the test, but any location (including a hospital) can be approved to assess clinical skills. Any person may work up to 120 days without certification in the three areas. With certification, typical per-hour pay is $5.25 for long-term care nurse aides and $8 for home health care aides.

Implementation and Administration

Students must pass the clinical skills test before taking the written test. Since July 1995, students have been required to complete seventy-five hours of classroom training and twelve hours of clinical training before taking either test. Students study the subjects identified in the Health Certification Project duty/task list developed by Oklahoma Vo-Tech. The test-development method is the same one the Oklahoma competency-based assessment system uses (described above).

There are forty-three test sites in Oklahoma. The tests must meet federal and state licensure requirements for the relevant occupation. It costs each student $30 to take the clinical skills test (the home health aide test is a little more expensive because it requires thirteen competencies). The fees collected go to the area vocational-technical schools. It also costs $30 to take the written test (the area vo-tech school keeps $5; Oklahoma Vo-Tech receives the remaining $25).

Oklahoma Vo-Tech is breaking even in administering the health tests.

The written exam is administered monthly; the clinical exam is by appointment (about six times per month). The performance assessments do not evaluate all the skills required to be competent for entry into the occupation. For example, in long-term care, only three skills are tested (selected randomly from fifty-two skills). In home health care, thirteen skills out of forty-eight are tested. It takes forty-five to sixty minutes to administer a clinical exam to one student, and each student is tested individually. Performance evaluators are trained using guides developed by Oklahoma Vo-Tech. Evaluators are paid about $19 an hour to observe and score the tests. The procedure for maintaining the quality of the multiple-choice portion of the exam is the same one used for the overall state competency-based system.

ASSOCIATED GENERAL CONTRACTORS NATIONAL CERTIFICATION

Description and Purpose

Because of Oklahoma's reputation for developing competency-based testing, AGC hired Oklahoma Vo-Tech to develop assessments and administer a program that leads to nationally recognized credentials in three areas of the construction industry: carpentry (commercial and residential), bricklaying, and stone masonry. These are advanced certificates, with required prequalification of either two years of work experience, or one year of work experience plus the completion of a vocational education program. Prequalification must be documented on the registration form before the test will be administered. Contracting occupations were included in the certification program, but occupations outside of AGC's "contracting" jurisdiction, such as plumbing and electrician work, were excluded.

AGC was incorporated in 1921 as a full-service construction association representing the needs of both open-shop and collective-bargaining contractors. It represents 8,000 general contracting firms and 24,500 associate and affiliate members; it has 101 chapters nationwide. Its mission is stated as follows: "AGC is dedicated to providing programs that promote high standards in the construction industry. AGC has designed this certification program to give prestige and recognition to individuals working in the industry." AGC accredits training programs in various contracting trades. Its members work mainly on commercial construction, where workers are most in demand. The incentive to sit for one of the certificates varies from chapter to chapter. AGC spends a lot of time teaching contractors that they need to invest in training for the incoming workforce.

The first AGC-sponsored tests were administered in 1989. Tests are multiple-choice, with high-level skills incorporated into test questions. Academic skills such as basic math and reading are included. Oral testing is offered by special arrangement. They have never had a request for a test in a language other than English.

Implementation and Administration

Using the process developed for Oklahoma's competency-based system, AGC's workforce development committee oversees the certification program, including development of the task lists and multiple-choice tests. This committee and subcommittees in each certificate area are made up of contractors, training instructors, foremen, and supervisors. Tests are administered through the 101 local AGC chapters across the country. Workers can be trained anywhere and then take the test. Curriculum materials have been developed and sold (on a voluntary basis) to various kinds of training programs (secondary and postsecondary vocational education programs, apprenticeship programs, and companies). In 1996, 700 tests were scanned and 65 to 70 percent met the minimum passing score of 70 percent.

Task lists are reviewed and revised annually by committees of AGC contractors (the committees are coordinated by Oklahoma Vo-Tech). The committees select a pool of questions generated from the task list. These questions are entered into a test bank, which has grown over time. A test is then generated from the test bank every year. Tests range from fifty to 100 questions, depending on the tasks. Data on how important each task is to the particular job are taken into consideration in test development. Committees review tasks, test questions, and curricula annually.

In addition to developing curriculum materials and administering the test bank through an AGC subcontract, Oklahoma Vo-Tech administers the tests through local chapters, scores completed tests, and conducts item analysis for AGC certifications. Oklahoma Vo-Tech has worked with AGC for twenty-five years; the last five have been highly focused on these certifications. AGC funds both a program coordinator and a secretary at Oklahoma Vo-Tech to run the testing program. AGC also employs a full-time curriculum developer at the curriculum center in Oklahoma. Oklahoma instructors can buy materials at cost, whereas AGC receives profits from sales in other states. Oklahoma Vo-Tech is responsible for marketing the curriculum materials and tests.

The annual testing process begins in September, when chapters are asked to identify cities for test sites that year. About a third of the chapters request participation. In January, promotional materials are sent to the chapters to advertise certification. Registration/test administration is $15 per person per test (an individual may take more than one test). The test is then administered in April. The program coordinator works with test coordinators at each chapter to set up the test site and hire test examiners. The required conditions for each test site (such as lighting) and test examiners (such as a resume describing their work in a construction occupation) are specified.

Scores are reported for regions and test sites if there are enough test-takers. Individual results are confidential and are sent only to the test-taker. This sometimes is a problem for employers, who may have paid for the test and expect access to the results. However, results are not shared without the permission of the test-taker. The program coordinator compiles a report for each chapter, with tips on how to improve scores next year.

Seventy percent is the minimum passing score on all tests. Research was done on the relationship between test score, skill level, and job performance, and the analysts decided (somewhat informally) that 70 percent was a "good" score for predicting successful job performance. However, there was no scientific research underlying this cutoff score.

AGC aims to break even financially by having registration and test fees balance the costs of the testing program. One way to do this is to have test sites recruit more test-takers (with a limit of twenty per site). Recruiting more test-takers may be difficult in some areas, however, because of limited incentives to take the test. Another way is to raise fees. When the program originally began, the committee thought the $15 fee would allow the program to break even or even make a profit. But even though money has been lost on the assessment program, no fee hikes have been considered, because the goal is to keep the tests affordable. Adding to the problem is the fact that originally there was national union resistance, so the program was more difficult to implement than anticipated. Currently, AGC has about forty test sites in twenty-five states.

The AGC system was designed to be economically affordable and legally defensible. All that is needed for a site to administer the exams is a test-form scanner and AGC's customized software. One of the main reasons AGC does not use more performance assessments is their high cost. In addition, case law suggests that test-takers may be tested on only those tasks required to perform on the job. Worried about costs and legal challenges, AGC has steered clear of developing or implementing performance assessments. Although there is only limited research to support them, the advisory committee and state staff believe that multiple-choice test scores are highly correlated with job performance and will stand up to potential legal challenges.

Technical Quality

The AGC certification system is held to the same quality standards as the Oklahoma competency system. Content validity is high because tests are closely linked to the competencies developed by industry. Administrators would like to do additional research on concurrent validity by checking the correlation between scores and performance. They do use item analyses to review individual questions, handing off to a review committee any items that are performing unusually. A decision may then be made to delete an item(s) and adjust scores before they are reported to individuals.

Consequences and Use of Assessment Results

Certificates can be used not only for hiring, but also to document advanced training for raises and promotions. AGC includes both unionized and nonunionized contractors. Union contractors utilize the apprenticeship system, whereas nonunion contractors operate an open shop, where employment is open to all regardless of qualifications. If a contractor hires only union members, certification can be used as an added qualification to help contractors decide which employees to hire; in some cases, employers are required to pay certified workers more. If it is an open shop, it is up to the contractor to decide how to use the certification. On average, 75 percent of the testers' fees are paid by employers.

AGC provides those who successfully complete certification with an identifying hard-hat decal, wall certificate, and pocket card. AGC hopes that these items will bestow prestige on completers in the eyes of the workers and contractors, and thus will encourage more interest in initial and advanced training. AGC also hopes that the certification program will improve the performance of workers and build pride in skilled craftsmanship.

TWO NEW CERTIFICATION INITIATIVES

In January 1996, the following two new certification initiatives were added.

Occupational Licensing Project

The Occupational Licensing Project (OLP) is the second to be jointly established with the Oklahoma Department of Health. The project is developing occupational duty/task lists and state licensing exams for the following areas: mechanical (sixteen licenses), electrical (four licenses), plumbing (four licenses), sanitarian (one license), fire alarm (two licenses), and burglar alarm (two licenses). The project is also developing a system that will allow the Oklahoma Department of Health to have on-site scanning and analysis capabilities. Until this segment of the project is complete, Oklahoma Vo-Tech is providing individual and group analysis as well as item analysis for these exams.

Vocational Teacher Certification Project

In July 1996, the testing division entered into a joint agreement with the Oklahoma Department of Education to oversee teacher certification for the following four vocational certification areas: agricultural eduation, family and consumer sciences, marketing education, and technology education.   This project involves development of duty/task lists and certification exams for each area, as well as co-ordination of the administration and analysis of these certification exams.

APPLICABILITY OF THE FIVE OKLAHOMA ASSESSMENTS TO VOCATIONAL EDUCATION

Over a period of ten years, the Oklahoma competency-based assessments have developed into a system that has a good reputation and continues to branch into new areas—specifically, the statewide health licensure, AGC certification, occupational licensure, and teacher certification. The administrative and quality control procedures for multiple-choice examinations are already in place, and this system has conducted some experimentation with performance-based assessment. Although Oklahoma Vo-Tech believes that performance-based assessment is not a viable option statewide (for financial and logistical reasons), it is having some success with its statewide health licensing system, which includes performance tasks. However, reliability and consistency are still issues in all of its assessments.

All of the assessment systems are applicable to vocational education, although with slightly different objectives and incentives for participation.   The Oklahoma competency-based assessment system started as a way to certify student skills and knowledge, as well as to move curriculum toward teaching skills and encourage instructional methods to focus more on student demonstrations of competency. However, many programs did not participate in the system. With the implementation of performance measures and standards, local sites are required to use the assessment system to report performance to the state and to make progress in program improvement. Many local instructors now see the system as "another state requirement" for accountability, rather than as a certification system for helping students.

Oklahoma education officials see a need not only to certify students' occupationally specific skills through their current system, but also to certify broader, more general skills through a "career passport," which students will complete and present to potential employers. State agency staff hope that once the passport system is implemented, educators will see passports and the vocational assessments as complementary parts of a certifying credential that students can use to gain employment. It is hoped that the passport system will be viewed by instructors as integral to their curriculum.

Of the assessment systems, the one for the six health certificates has had the most success in combining multiple-choice and performance-based assessments. It has also been the most successful in breaking even on administration costs and recruiting test-takers. The health certifications are required for licensure, which is necessary for employment, and demand in these fields has been steady, especially in home care occupations.

The AGC assessment system was developed to provide advanced certification (not entry-level employment) in three areas of the construction industry. At this point, the program is not recruiting enough test-takers to break even. The incentives for participation are based on demand and the strength of unions (and unions' preferred uses for the certification), which vary by locale. Therefore, participation rates differ considerably. The occupational areas being certified are not licensed professions, so participation is left to the discretion of employers, who decide based on market conditions and observed employee performance. Employers that hire both union and nonunion employees must value the certificate and incorporate it into hiring practices and salary scales if AGC is to increase participation.

One process for developing an assessment has been adapted for the other assessment systems. The five systems have slightly different objectives and participants, but all are a part of the vocational education enterprise. For the most part, what can be learned from these cases is how to administer, nationally or statewide, criterion-referenced, competency-based, multiple-choice tests, with more limited lessons on locally designed and administered performance-based assessment. In many ways, vocational education in Oklahoma is atypical. The state strongly supports vocational education with numerous state staff and substantial funding. It operates with an entrepreneurial spirit not common in state bureaucracies. Consistent leadership and staff, university support, and a tradition of strong vocational education programs statewide have worked in Oklahoma's favor. If they lack one or more of these elements, other states or metropolitan areas that try to adopt this system or develop a similar one may encounter problems.

VOCATIONAL/INDUSTRIAL CLUBS OF AMERICA
NATIONAL COMPETITION

DESCRIPTION AND PURPOSE

Vocational/Industrial Clubs of America (VICA) is a national organization for secondary and postsecondary students in vocational/technical fields. The occupationally oriented skills tests that form the centerpiece of VICA's national conference, called the Skills USA Championships, cover a broad range of vocational fields, test generic and job-specific skills, and use several different forms of assessment. VICA, a nonprofit organization, has obtained assistance from corporate leaders and practitioners in some sixty fields to develop its tests, which are designed to measure skills required in those fields anywhere in the nation. The main purposes of VICA's contests are to document students' skill mastery, encourage excellence, and increase the competence of entry-level workers. Indirectly, VICA also aims to improve instruction and curriculum.

There are two main types of contests, the *job skills contests*, in which individuals compete in performing job-related skills and applying relevant knowledge from the vocational field they are studying, and the *leadership development contests*, which consist mainly of demonstrating generic and employment-readiness skills, but also include more academic skills, such as speech making and knowledge of parliamentary procedure. The national competition is the culmination of local, district, and state contests in which winners proceed to the next higher level.

The VICA assessments focus mainly on demonstrating hands-on occupationally specific skills. Many, however, also call for cluster-focused or more general, industrywide knowledge (such as fundamentals of electronics, in the electronic products servicing contest); generic-thinking, decision-making, or troubleshooting/diagnostic skills (e.g., in automotive repair technology); or specific academic skills (e.g., math skills in cabinetmaking).

In many of the contest areas, a written exam is included; items are usually multiple choice, but sometimes are constructed response. The different components are designed to test the skills and knowledge a person needs to work in a specific occupation or occupational group, so the parts are intended to complement one another. Figure F.1 gives detailed descriptions of several job skills tests.

Test results are used to determine first-, second-, and third-place winners in each competition among secondary students and then among postsecondary students.[1] The winners are determined by the total scores on all components, or contest stations, from all judges. Many times, the scores are so close that a fraction of one point (out of a score typically in three digits) determines who wins. The top three scorers in each category (secondary and post-secondary) win medals and prizes such as scholarships and equipment. (Other participants are given certificates.) Each first-place winner in a skill area that is also part of the international competition in which VICA participates gets to compete in a runoff against the winner in that skill area from the previous year. Runoff winners then receive additional in-depth industry-sponsored training to prepare for the international competition.

The contests are judged using criterion-referenced scoring. In most cases, contests combine objective questions that have a single right answer (e.g., a multiple-choice, yes/no, or mathematical question) with aesthetic or subjective judgments about student progress (e.g., in cosmetology, advertising design, culinary arts, and even in skill areas such as cabinetmaking and precision machining). In some cases, points are awarded for overall quality of a project, introducing a holistic element to the scores.

---

[1]These two categories are ranked separately, even though the contests, with only rare exceptions, involve the same tasks.

The vocational-technical areas represented in the skills contests range from trade and industrial crafts (auto mechanics, brick masonry, carpentry, printing) to home economics–related or service occupations (culinary arts, commercial sewing, cosmetology, practical nursing, advertising design) to emerging or rapidly changing technology-based occupations (automated manufacturing technology, robotic workcell technology). Some leadership development assessments pit teams of students against each other, but most require strictly individual performances. Brief descriptions of the specific tasks assigned for a few of the assessments follow.

Electronic Products Servicing

The contest consists of three main parts: assembling an electronic product following a schematic drawing, diagnosing the malfunctioning component in several products and identifying an appropriate repair strategy, and completing a written exam on electronics facts and theory. The contestant must demonstrate safety procedures throughout the contest. Associated skills that are needed to perform these tasks include selecting appropriate test equipment, following safety procedures, soldering and desoldering, and performing tasks quickly (as well as correctly).

Law Enforcement

A written test covers constitutional and criminal law, main principles of the U.S. criminal justice system, rules of evidence, the law enforcement code of ethics, and similar topics. Contestants also must respond to video-supported scenarios involving, for example, an armed robbery in progress (including facing the split-second decision of whether to shoot at suspects). They must follow proper procedures in conducting an initial investigation of a threatening situation, make an arrest, collect evidence, and fill out an evidence collection form.

Culinary Arts

There are two separate contests, one for secondary and the other (more difficult) for postsecondary. In each, students must prepare several platters of cold foods and a multicourse meal of hot/cooked items using ingredients, equipment, and tools provided. Judging covers the following elements: sanitation and safety; *mise en place* (visual presentation), organizational skill, technical skills (chopping, slicing, sautéing, kneading dough, etc.), quality of prepared items (taste and smell), and creativity.

Precision Machining Technology

A range of projects includes: milling a piece of aluminum or turning on a lathe to specifications in a blueprint (two separate tasks); interpreting a blueprint and answering questions; technical sketching; bench work, including layout, deburring, assembly, filing, drilling, grinding, hacksawing, and fitting; making calculations using gauge blocks; and implementing precision measurement (micrometer variations and transfer measurement).

Figure F.1—Some Specific Contests

Advertising Design/Commercial Art

There are three main components. Students must 1) compose a camera-ready mechanical (pasteup) according to specs for a print ad using manual methods and tools, including laying out the type, placing amberlith for photo position, cropping photos, and drawing a ruled box; 2) compose another mechanical using PageMaker software according to specs; and 3) design an advertising or graphic product, including generating content ideas and executing them for several thumbnail sketches, several "roughs" (more developed than thumbnails), and one finished product, according to instructions provided. One recent year's creative project assigned a cover and first page for a children's cookbook; this year's was a table-top (tent-style) ad for a restaurant.

Carpentry

Contestants construct an element of a building, such as a stair stringer or a wall with a window, following blueprint instructions for the main part of this contest. The other part is a written test that requires identifying tools, calculating relevant measures (e.g., cubic yards of concrete to fill a given space), and demonstrating general knowledge of accepted practices.

Practical Nursing

Tasks may include: obtaining/recording vital signs; changing a wound dressing; making an occupied bed; performing cardiopulmonary resuscitation and emergency cardiac care intervention; and preparing, administering, and recording medication following a doctor's instructions.

Job Skills Demonstrations (in Leadership Development contests)

Students demonstrate a job skill that can be explained briefly. The goal is to teach the judges how to do the skill, so students must actually demonstrate it while explaining how to do it. Components that are judged include organization of the presentation (including the presence of an appropriate introduction and conclusion); poise; clarity and grammar; diction, speed, control, and tone of voice; and overall content.

Figure F.1—continued

The leadership development competition goes on for several days and includes the opening and closing ceremonies (group competitions that test public speaking, organization, synchronized movement, and memorization). The job skills contests take place during a single day. Competitors do not find out who won until the last night. At the awards ceremony, first-, second-, and third-place winners are announced in front of the thousands of conference participants, family members, and guests; they then go to the podium to receive their medals (gold, silver, and bronze; respectively). *All* contestants receive a certificate for having competed, and the other top-ten finishers (those who place fourth through tenth in each contest) receive special recognition on their certificates.

The tests are all developed by technical committees. For the leadership development contests, these committees consist mainly of vocational-technical teachers; for the job skills tests, committee members are current or former professionals in the particular occupation or industry, along with some people who work for a relevant industry association or labor union. Only these industry representatives set standards and design assessments, but other committee functions (such as running the contests) may be performed by teachers as well.

The technical committees develop the tests through a series of meetings and conference calls; they solicit feedback from teachers about the feasibility of new assessment ideas. The process is somewhat informal and varies considerably from one skill area to another. In a very few areas—automechanics, electronics, precision machining, and technical drafting—the committees have used the standards produced by national skill standards development groups to guide their test content. The committees may draw on task lists for an occupation or on tests developed at the state or local level, changing test questions substantially to prevent unfair advantage going to one or another state's competitors.[2]

The people who participated in the job skills contests as competitors, judges, technical advisors, education team members (for liaison and communication), and advisors/chaperones were in general quite positive and enthusiastic about the VICA program and the system of job skills contests, including the local, state, and national competitions. While it is not surprising that students who had won local and state competitions were excited about attending the national conference, it is more telling that high-level managers and other employees in the industries VICA serves were strong supporters of the program. Many have been involved year after year in designing the tests, working out logistics, or judging the competitions, and many were taking personal time off from their jobs to do this work (entailing several days to a week of very long hours). If there are any downsides

---

[2]During an interview at the VICA Skills USA Championships, one technical committee member reported that to guard against possible cheating, a half-hour before a test began he changed a factual element (the type of metal, in automated manufacturing technology) that would change many of the calculations students needed to do. (This interview and all others at the competition were conducted anonymously.)

to VICA's contests, they were not apparent at the Skills USA Championships.

In some cases, this dedication may reflect appreciation for VICA's having helped them at the start of their careers, but it also attests to positive impressions of VICA's ongoing work; it seems unlikely that so many professionals would continue to work on the conference and persuade their companies to donate equipment and materials if they were not consistently recruiting good employees through VICA. Industry representatives, mainly managers or laborers in the skilled trades, are complemented by industry association employees, vocational teachers (secondary and postsecondary), labor union representatives, and vocational administrators (school or local/state agency) in putting together this wide-ranging conference.

The contests contribute significantly to VICA's overall goal, which is to prepare qualified and highly motivated workers, mostly for occupations in the skilled trade and industrial sectors, some of whom go on to become managers and leaders in these sectors. In preparing for the contests and working with teachers who have access to VICA's other offerings, students should gain not only the practical knowledge demanded by their industry, but generic workplace qualities and skills needed for entry to and success in any industry (such as dependability and integrity, and teamwork, decision-making, and communication skills). The contests are just one part of VICA's overall program, which also includes teacher training workshops, publications, and access to personal networks in industry.

RELATIONSHIP TO OTHER PROGRAMS

VICA aims for its contests to be closely related to instruction in classes taught by VICA members, though these ties undoubtedly vary across competition fields and across instructors. The tests seem to drive the curriculum content more than they respond to it. The skills and knowledge tested by VICA's Skills USA Championships should in most cases also have been tested earlier, in the classroom, though the national contests may serve as a kind of final or comprehensive exam, not just for one course but for a program or group of related courses. VICA's contests bring together more content elements than a typical school test does, and may use more current or cutting-edge technology than some schools have. (This can be a problem, because some students will be less prepared than others through no fault of their own.) VICA distributes the topics for next year's leadership contests in advance to teachers and student members, so they have a good idea what to emphasize. Previous year's project plans are released to familiarize teachers with contest procedures and to aid the planning of local and state contests. Moreover, the specific competencies that will be tested are listed in the official technical standards, which are revamped every three years.

In most of the skill areas, training seminars are offered to teacher members through the state VICA offices on a regular basis. These seminars serve at least two purposes: keeping teachers informed about changes in the industry or occupation and new curricular or teaching materials, and gathering data from teachers about topics on which they need more information. At these sessions, teachers can discover tasks that may be useful in their own classroom tests and discuss curriculum and instructional issues with others from around the state (or country, since seminars are also given at the national conferences). Teachers also have opportunities to make contacts with industry representatives for field trips, internships, and mentorship opportunities. Teachers may even be able to earn college or inservice training credits by taking a lead role in running the state VICA competition or teaching continuing education seminars.

The links between classroom/workshop instruction and these national contests mean that students at the national competition should be familiar with the format of the tests *and* should know in advance what content areas will be tested. For one thing, those who make it to the nationals have usually won in the same area earlier in the school year at their state competition.[3] In addition, teachers are supposed to have the official technical standards, which provide specific information about the competencies that the national contests

---

[3]The official rules state that only first-place winners from the state competitions go on to compete in the nationals, except that if a first-place winner is unable to attend, the competitor with the next highest score takes his or her place. Discussions with teachers/advisors indicated that a similar sifting process is supposed to occur in going from local/district competitions to the state level. However, in practice a small proportion of competitors have not had adequate preparation for the national contests, either because of weak competition in their state or because they did not win in their state but were asked to represent it due to unusual circumstances.

may test. However, in practice many teachers do not have the current version. This problem was especially common among teachers who taught contestants in the leadership development areas. This lack of initiative on the part of some teachers is mystifying, given that the offical standards cost only $10 and are updated only once in three years.

IMPLEMENTATION AND ADMINISTRATION

The VICA contests started in the mid-1960s with only three contest areas (all in leadership development) and have grown steadily since then. The national job skills and leadership development events now involve thousands of students in dozens of competitions. These assessments are implemented annually from the local to the international level. (Only certain areas are competed in internationally, the choice depending on the presence of strong programs in enough participating countries. Skill areas differ among the other levels of competition as well.) VICA members in the state hosting the national conference, especially the teachers, play a stronger role than members from other states.

The specific content of tests is changed every year, though most of the subject material covered remains consistent from one year to the next. Students can compete in events for more than one year so long as they still meet the eligibility requirements, so VICA has to change the tests to keep things fair. Students must be active VICA members to compete, and must compete during the school year in which they are enrolled in a course or program in the same subject area as the competition (for local, regional, and state competitions) or at the end of that year, in June (for the national competition). Tests used at the national level are released for use by state, regional, and local competitions in subsequent years; these are usually modified and shortened to suit the state and local contests, which generally are finished within one day. Teachers can also obtain these tests for use in their classrooms.

Judges for the job skills tests are (or recently were) professionals in the relevant field, i.e., they perform or supervise the tasks being tested or set standards in the occupational field. Judges for the leadership development contests are teachers or professionals in the relevant field. All judges receive training in what to look for, how to score, how to strategize in assigning scores so that there is room above a strong performer for an even better or perfect score, and so on. To encourage consistency in judging, new judges are always put on a team with experienced judges and encouraged to ask questions; the new judge's work is carefully monitored by the experienced judges. All judges attend a "familiarization session" for contests that have new equipment, computers, software, or a dramatically different test element; these sessions can last up to a full day. The extensiveness of the judges' training varies from one field to another, but no one interviewed suggested that the judges received less than adequate training.

As to the fairness of the judging, people interviewed thought that each judge was fairly consistent across the projects he or she judged, even though there could be a wide variation across judges' scores for one contestant or on one test component. Since the scores used for ranking contestants are the totals from all judges, one judge being consistently lenient should not affect the relative position of any contestant. In some contests, one highly experienced judge scores all contestants' products or papers for a component of the test. One line of thinking is that VICA student members should get used to judging that may be subjective, since such judgments occur on the job. National VICA staff say that there has been general acclaim for the fairness of the contest judging—but there are no hard data, such as external reviews from unbiased experts, to confirm this.

TECHNICAL QUALITY

No research has been done on the validity, reliability, or equity of VICA's assessments (either test content or methods). VICA has kept electronic records of the score results from the national contests for the last five to six years, so some of the data needed to do such research exist. However, there has not been sufficient demand for it to be done.

Validity

Those involved with VICA believe that the tests are highly valid because industry is extensively involved in designing them. Industry representatives work hard on many different tasks at the conference and on activities during the year leading up to it; they also secure funds and equipment. Their motivation is to produce future workers who may contribute to their company's success, so they want to make the tests fair, challenging, up-to-date, and authentic. Teachers also work hard, because they want to improve their students' chances for success. The result is that everyone involved has strong, consistent motivations.

There are contests in which logistical or other difficulties tend to obstruct the fairness of test administration, however. These are probably fairly rare occurrences that usually happen when a skill area is completely new or a new element is introduced to an existing contest. For example, in this year's advertising design contest, four problems led to unfair advantage for certain contestants in the view of one teacher/advisor. First, the technical committee did not allow adequate time or opportunity for competitors to clarify the meaning of terms they had not heard before (they may have been familiar with the concept but by another name). Allowing such discussion adds authenticity to the experience, since an ad agency employee would normally be able to clarify what the client wants before proceeding.

The other three problems had to do with the fact that part of the competition was done on computers at a local school. First, and perhaps most significant, students who were familiar with the software used at that particular school had a distinct advantage, especially since it was a timed project.[4] Second, some of the printers failed to work properly, wasting time for some students but not others. Third, a class was being conducted in another part of the room where some contestants were working, causing distraction—but for only some students.

---

[4]One could argue that if schools want to prepare their students for work, they should have up-to-date computers and use the software most commonly used in the field, but obviously a given student's having worked on specific software is a matter of access and not a reflection of his or her abilities. Information about what software will be used is published in April, but some students may not have access to the right type of equipment to obtain adequate practice.

Reliability

Informants believed judges' scores were adequately reliable. Whenever possible, judges are given objective criteria to use in making decisions about correctness of responses or performances. In cases where subjective judgment enters into the score (particularly in aesthetic areas such as how pleasing or effective a graphic design or advertising concept is, or how food looks and tastes), there is probably more variation among the judges' scores. However, these differences likely even out in the total scores (assuming that judges are consistent across the different contestants). Informants did not feel a need to formally measure the reliability of the scores.

People running the contests strive for fairness. On one troubleshooting component of the electronic product servicing event, some of the contestants had a faulty reading on a diagnostic tool and thought this was the problem they were being asked to identify. Although the person who designed this part of the test thought they should have known this was not the intended problem, and said so at the debriefing, the technical committee eliminated that part of the test after several contestants filed a grievance to challenge their scores.

Debriefings are held in many contest areas to go over the correct answers, section by section, and discuss how contestants performed in the aggregate. At these sessions, students can learn from what they did wrong (and, to some degree, satisfy their curiosity about what their chances of winning are). Some of the debriefings stuck to the points raised in the contests; others involved long-winded presentations of new materials and equipment, amounting to endorsements/advertising for a company's products (in exchange for the items and/or labor the company donated to the conference). This by-product of the contests' corporate sponsorship is unfortunate, but it is of minor importance compared with what the contests offer in opportunities to excel, to learn from others, and to discover more about employment and postsecondary training options.

Equity

Everyone asked about this issue said that it was not possible for a person's gender or race/ethnicity to influence judges of the job skills tests, since in many cases judges fill out the scoring sheets for the whole group of products after contestants have departed, and these are identified only by contestant number. However, in most of the job skills areas, the vast majority of the contestants were either white males or white females. In such a setting, the one or two contestants who do not fit the pattern (e.g., the one female welder among a group of males) may in fact stick in the judges' minds, since judges usually observe the performances as well. Thus, there may be subconscious bias either favoring or disfavoring students who stand out from the group. In some trade areas, the groups were more mixed, especially by gender (e.g., advertising design and culinary arts).

In all of the leadership development tests except those few that involve teams (such as parliamentary/chapter business procedure), judges observe the contestants one by one as they perform, so one cannot argue that the procedures preclude bias. It is therefore possible for unfair judging based on gender or race/ethnicity to occur, though no one asked about this was aware of any such instance. It is also quite possible for judges to take into consideration additional factors beyond the skills and attributes tested, such as appearance or voice characteristics, whether consciously or not.

CONSEQUENCES AND USE OF ASSESSMENT RESULTS

For the most part, results are used only informally by students, teachers, and employers. The following discussion addresses these groups separately.

Students

Though the goal is to share students' results with them, the students may have graduated from high school or their postsecondary program just before competing in June and may not be in touch with their teachers during the summer. Although scores and rankings are given to all state VICA advisors at the close of the awards session, in some cases they are not disseminated further to teachers or students. The actual results are not used for formal decisions about a competitor's schooling or employment. However, individual student competitors use the experience of preparing and participating in various ways: to make contacts for jobs or further training, to help decide on particular avenues to pursue within an industry or job category (e.g., whether to strive to be a charge nurse, who manages other nurses in a unit), to bolster his or her resume, to learn to handle pressure, and to learn skills or helpful tricks from other competitors' performances.[5]

Student participants reported increased enthusiasm for schoolwork, higher self-confidence and aspirations, more assertiveness, gains in teamwork skills (for some events), and better decision-making ability. Results mentioned by students were generally quite positive. On the downside, some students experience anxiety or disappointment if they do not win, and a small minority even show temporary symptoms of illness from the stress. A small percentage of students are unpleasantly surprised to discover that industry standards represented at the VICA conference are higher (or cover different content) than standards at their school or at the state competitions. A small proportion of students interviewed mentioned that they found it difficult to deal with strains on friendships when they won a contest but a good friend did not, especially when they were in direct competition with the friend (this is far more likely at the state and local competitions). These negative effects are minimal, however, compared with the substantial positive effects cited by all students interviewed.

Students from different backgrounds may gain different benefits from participating in the contests. An outstanding high school student in a college-prep or other highly rigorous program may sharpen his or her interpersonal, communication, and public-speaking skills through contest preparation or other chapter activities. An average student in a general or vocational track may get involved in electronics or machining through VICA, do well and gain confidence, take more math classes, and decide to enroll in a technically oriented college program. There are even limited roles for developmentally disabled or other special-needs students: the custodial services competition is restricted to students with individual educational plans. Several student competitors at the 1995 competition had a physical disability. Teachers thought that most students possessed a

---

[5]Students are more likely to have time to observe others in the leadership development events, where they can observe each competitor who follows their own performance, and in job skills tests that take relatively little time to complete and have more than one batch of competitors. In job skills tests that take most of the day, students have little or no time for observation.

high degree of motivation before deciding to participate, but in a few cases the rewards offered by the VICA program may have reached out to at-risk students. For example, one teacher of law enforcement/criminal justice issues from a poor, small-town school in Texas said he had used the lure of a steady job and higher chances of entering postsecondary school to turn around some potential gang members.

Teachers

Teachers are supposed to receive the individual scores for the students competing from their program (one per skill area). They also should receive scores for each state's national competitors and the national average and standard deviation of the national scores. Some teachers reported that they received information from their state director in a form that was difficult to understand; others never received the scores. (What is reported to teachers after the state and local competitions undoubtedly varies too.) Teachers who receive readable results can see which skills they are teaching well or not so well, based on how their students compare nationally.

However, to make sound judgments about how they may need to change their curriculum, teaching methods, or equipment, teachers really need additional information—for example, a description or example of the ideal performance sought by the judges, whether the student was particularly nervous and did not perform up to potential, or whether another instructional factor harmed the student's performance (e.g., the school lacks a particular software program or type of equipment). At least one skill area, precision machining technology, provides a detailed report that explains each item or element at each workstation, including the perfect answer or product the judges were looking for and an overview of how students as a group performed in each station's activities (reporting subscore averages).

Teachers who observe the job skills contests may begin thinking about ways in which to change their teaching if they find that industry demands skills they were not previously teaching or emphasizing sufficiently. Teachers can benefit from this knowledge whether or not they attend the national conference, either by discussing test content with participating colleagues or with contestants who report back from the conference, or by obtaining tests used in previous years. Teachers are likely to revise their definition of acceptable performance (generally by raising their standards) after experiencing the VICA competition. They are somewhat less likely to change teaching methods, because instruction is not discussed or modeled at the conference (though they may learn new techniques informally by discussing them with other teachers).

Teaching to the test was a common effect of being involved with VICA, but since the tests are thought to reflect the knowledge and skills that industry wants, this was seen as beneficial.[6]

Teachers who join VICA may attend seminars with industry representatives and statewide meetings at which they gain access to a range of benefits:

- Curricular materials that focus on developing leadership and communication skills among the students, encouraging community service work, and improving attitudes toward school and work. In certain industries, national associations have produced new curricular materials—e.g., *Raising the Standard* (Electronic Industries Association and Electronic Industries Foundation, 1994) in electronic products servicing.

- Access to industry contacts and the opportunity to hear about new equipment and techniques, skills being sought by industry, and even labor market information.

- Continuing education credits, for those who take a leadership role in helping to write or pretest an assessment, soliciting support from industry, or planning for or managing a local or state conference.

Employers

Some employers send representatives to the VICA competitions. These representatives attend partly to recruit employees and may

---

[6]It is noteworthy that some teachers, especially for some of the leadership development contests, apparently did not read the specific contest regulations carefully, or at all, and so were not in a position to teach their students to prepare well for the tests.

talk to students they have seen performing especially well. Employers do not receive student scores from VICA, but they have access to the list of winners.

APPLICABILITY TO VOCATIONAL EDUCATION

The costs of putting together a national compettiton such as VICA's are enormous. They cover three main areas: equipment, materials, and facilities; labor for contest design, setup, judging, and break-down; and personal transportation to the conference site. Most of these costs would not be incurred if a school or district were to im-plement a similar assessment locally. The equipment required would presumably be available at the school; however, school-owned equipment would probably not be as up-to-date and possibly would be less sophisticated or useful than what is available at the national conference (all of which is donated or loaned to VICA for the event). Materials beyond what a school's budget covers would likely need to be located for a competition (or in-class testing), either by purchase or by soliciting donations from industry. The substantial facilities costs, which VICA pays for the national competition (conference center rental, provision of plumbing connections and special ventilation ducts, electricity use, catering for certain events, etc.), could be avoided at local competitions. The costs of personal transportation (which in VICA's case are paid for by students, their families, school fund-raisers, supporting firms, and school/district funds, especially for teachers' travel) would also be mainly avoided.

The most substantial obstacle in replicating these assessments in schools is replacing the labor involved, especially for test design and judging. Although this labor is all contributed by professionals in the fields being tested and teachers, so there is no dollar amount that needs to be covered, it is unlikely that a local contest could begin to replicate this level of expertise. A key aspect of VICA job skills contests is that the judging is done by expert practitioners, giving both students and teachers a more realistic and current view of the performance expected in the industry than they would get having teachers as judges. Moreover, since the level of competition is bound to be higher with the larger, national pool of contestants, students may not work as hard to prepare for a local event. Knowing who their competition is (which would be the case if competition is restricted to their class, and may be the case if the competition is schoolwide) or sensing that the competition is not very fierce may keep students from putting in the same effort they would expend for a national competition.

However, despite these obstacles, the content of the tests can be useful to individual teachers and groups of teachers meeting to revise their courses or programs. The judging sheets are available in the Skills USA Championships technical standards (revised once every three years), and tests given at the nationals are released for use at state and district level competitions in subsequent years. The input from industry should also provide an important lesson for all vocational educators: even if it is not possible to command the high level of commitment from industry representatives that VICA does in designing and implementing these assessments, schools should seek and use industry's viewpoints and knowledge wherever possible.

(especially in "high performance" work environments) and have determined that the knowledge of experts in a particular field is often highly integrated and situational. Instead of viewing jobs as a list of decontextualized skills or abilities, researchers are beginning to describe the actions of workers as performances in response to situations (Wirt, 1995). In addition, experts gain and use information by working with others and creating shared knowledge to be used in the workplace. For example, although a dental technician and a vocational nurse both need to communicate with other health care professionals in their jobs, the nature of their communication differs because the structure of their work teams differs. Furthermore, as frontline workers become more autonomous and are given greater responsibility for decision making, they play a greater role in shaping the nature of the work they perform (Berryman and Bailey, 1992). Employers are seeking individuals who can adapt to changing workplace conditions, communicate and work effectively with others, and solve problems. These are not skills that can be learned from a book or in pieces in a classroom; they require opportunities to perform in realistic settings.

This perspective on skills demands a different approach to instruction and assessment. Large units of performance become the focal point, and the units are "situated" in a realistic context such as might be encountered on the job. For example, students competing in a VICA contest typically are not asked to list the steps to be performed when taking an order from a client; instead they are asked to hold a realistic conversation with a person acting as client and are judged on how well they perform. Similarly, the work samples that students include in their C-TAP portfolios document performance of an occupational task in a real-world setting. Vocational assessments are becoming more highly situated, and most of the assessments we sampled emphasized authentic performance of complex behaviors in real-world settings.

Table 3

Knowledge and Skills Assessed in the Sample

Assessment Activity	General Workforce Preparation	Industry Core Skills and Knowledge	Occupational Skills	Specific Occupational Skills
Career-Technical Assessment Program (C-TAP)	✓	✓ (optional)	✓	✓ (optional)
Kentucky Instructional Results Information System (KIRIS)	✓			
Laborers-AGC environmental training and certification programs				✓
National Board for Professional Teaching Standards (NBPTS) certification program			✓	
Oklahoma competency-based testing program	✓			✓
Vocational / Industrial Clubs of America (VICA) national competition	✓			✓

NOTE: Oklahoma is phasing in assessments of occupational cluster skills.

skills related to printed material. For example, a student enrolled in a nursing course may need to learn terminology and record-keeping skills that can be assessed well with multiple-choice and short-answer tests. However, there are other skills (many from other parts of the continuum) for which such tests are less well suited. The same student may also need to be able to work as part of an integrated health care team, a skill not as well assessed with pencil-and-paper methods. As discussed in the next chapter, alternative assessments may be more effective at measuring some vocational skills, including work skills more broadly defined.

The second change in thinking about vocational skills concerns the importance of the work context (Stasz et al., 1996). Cognitive scientists have begun to look at what people actually do in the workplace

or occupation-specific skills intended to help individuals prepare for workforce entry. Occupational cluster and specific occupational skills describe progressively more focused sets of skills that a worker needs to master for a job within a group of related occupations or a specific occupational field.

Traditionally, vocational educators in the United States have focused on skills at the latter, narrow end of this continuum and have organized training programs around them. In this approach, occupational responsibilities are decomposed into distinct, separable components that become the basis for the curriculum. For example, the trade of welding might be broken down into fifty to 100 distinct skills that are taught and practiced one at a time. This model for analyzing the demands of an occupation (called the *job competency model*) predominates in occupational training, occupational certification and licensing, and in the military (Wirt, 1995). A detailed inventory of component skills serves as the basis for training and assessment. Instructors or supervisors "check off" one by one those tasks that a person can perform and indicate one by one at what skill level they can be performed. The Oklahoma Vo-Tech assessment system is based on detailed task analyses of this type.

In recent years, however, employers have begun to seek less job-specific training and more general-workforce preparation. This shift from specific to general training reflects changes in the workplace due to technological progress and international competition. Secondary and postsecondary vocational programs are responding by developing programs that teach both broad and specific skills and that integrate academic and vocational knowledge. Federal law (U.S. Congress, 1990) mandates greater integration of academic and vocational education and an emphasis on "all aspects of the industry," so attention to the more generic skills is a growing priority for vocational education. Table 3 shows a breakdown of our sample of assessment systems based on the specificity of knowledge and skills addressed.

The type of knowledge and skills to be assessed can affect the choice of assessment methods, although there is no one-to-one correspondence between skill types and assessment types. Traditional assessment forms, including multiple-choice and short-answer questions, are efficient ways to measure factual knowledge and application of standards. Finally, aggregated information about student progress (acquired knowledge and skills, success in courses, etc.) is used to judge the quality of vocational programs. Although a single assessment may be used for many purposes—for example, standardized test results are used by teachers to identify individual student weaknesses and target instruction, and they are used by legislators and the general public to judge the quality of the state education system—it may not be equally effective for them all. Therefore, the choice of assessment should be made with the three possible broad uses of the information clearly in mind.

The most common reason for assessing students is to measure their individual progress as a means of improving instruction and promoting learning. Through direct observation and a variety of formal and informal assessment strategies, teachers keep track of what students learn, which instructional approaches work, and where changes need to be made. To be most helpful for these purposes, assessments should provide detailed information on the specific knowledge and skills that have been taught in the class. They should be administered often and graded quickly, and information should be provided to teachers and students so that adjustments can be made. Such assessments can be either on-demand or cumulative. Since teachers use the assessment results in conjunction with other knowledge of student performance, less of a premium needs to be placed on technical quality.

The demands change when assessments are used to verify that students have mastered a particular set of skills or body of knowledge. Assessment for mastery may focus on general abilities (such as for college admission) or specific skills (such as for professional licensing). The results are used for decisions about selection, placement, promotion, and certification. Because of the importance of these actions, extra attention must be paid to the quality of the measures, including their reliability, validity, and fairness. In many cases, mastery testing is based on multiple rather than single measures to increase the validity of the results.

Assessment can also be used to provide information about the quality of programs, schools, and districts that are providing education and training. This accountability may be based on individual performance or on group performance (e.g., a class or school). When

Chapter Two

THE ASSESSMENT CHALLENGE FACING VOCATIONAL EDUCATION

The process of selecting or developing an assessment begins with an examination of the intended uses of the assessment results. The first section of this chapter explores the purposes of vocational assessment and classifies the case studies of alternative assessment systems by purpose. Then, because vocational assessments must take into account the characteristics of the students being educated and the nature of the content being presented, the second section explores recent changes in the context of vocational education and their implications for assessment.

PURPOSES

Educational assessments can serve a variety of purposes, and the choice of assessment depends in part on how the assessment information will be used. There are three broad uses for educational assessment, all of which are relevant to vocational education (U.S. Congress, Office of Technology Assessment, 1992):

- To improve learning and instruction

- To certify individual mastery

- To evaluate program success

Vocational teachers use the results of tests and other assessments to monitor the progress of students, diagnose their needs, and make instructional plans. When students complete courses or sequences of courses, vocational programs use assessments to certify that students have achieved a required level of mastery or have met industry

constructed-response alternatives, including performance tasks, senior projects, and portfolios. Chapter Four discusses the quality and feasibility of alternative assessments. Chapter Five identifies other issues, such as standardization, consequences, and voluntariness, that are relevant to choosing appropriate assessment strategies, and summarizes the advantages associated with particular choices. Chapter Six presents examples of the kinds of assessment decisions confronting vocational educators and shows how the results of this study can contribute to those decisions. Six appendices are also provided, each describing one of the case studies in detail.

Vocational/Industrial Clubs of America National Competition

Vocational/Industrial Clubs of America (VICA) is a national organization for secondary and postsecondary students in some sixty vocational/technical fields. VICA conducts the Skills USA Championships, a national competition that focuses on performing occupationally specific skills in realistic contexts. Many of the skill areas include a written exam as well. The national competition is the culmination of local, regional, and state contests; winners proceed to the next level. The main purpose of the contests is to document students' skill mastery, encourage excellence, and improve the workforce. VICA also aims to improve curriculum and instruction. Performance in the contests is judged by experienced industry practitioners using specific task-related criteria. The organization places high priority on fairness and consistency in judging; however, no research has been done on the validity, reliability, or equity of the test content or scoring methods. VICA aims for its contests to be closely tied to instruction in the relevant field, though the closeness of the tie varies across competition fields and across instructors. Industry practitioners develop the performance tasks and the written tests under VICA's guidance. This extensive industry involvement increases the relevance of the assessments to the workplace. Students and teachers gain a reality-based and up-to-date picture of the performance and skills expected in their industry from the involvement of practitioners. The written tests are primarily multiple choice, but there are a few open-ended items as well. The VICA model would be relatively easy to replicate in schools. The most substantial obstacle would be recruiting experienced and knowledgeable industry people to design and judge the competitions.

ORGANIZATION

The rest of this report is organized as follows. Chapter Two examines the primary purposes served by assessments in education and the two specific conditions that are generating demands for alternative methods of assessment among vocational educators: the changing student population and the rapidly evolving skill mix that must be reflected in vocational programs. Chapter Three describes the range of assessment methods, from common multiple-choice tests to new

Multiple-choice tests are quite efficient. Students answer numerous questions in a small amount of time. With the advent of optical mark sensors, responses can be scored and reported extremely quickly and inexpensively. Such tests provide an efficient means of gathering information about a wide range of knowledge and skills. Multiple-choice tests are not restricted to factual knowledge; they can also be used to measure many kinds of higher-order thinking and problem-solving skills. However, considerable skill is required to develop test items that measure analysis, evaluation, and other higher cognitive skills.

The other two types of written assessment both involve constructed responses. The first consists of open-ended questions requiring short written answers. The required answer might be a word or phrase (such as the name of a particular piece of equipment), a sentence or two (such as a description of the steps in a specific procedure), or a longer written response (such as an explanation of how to apply particular knowledge or skills to a situation). In the simplest case, short-answer questions make very limited cognitive demands, asking students to produce specific knowledge or facts. In other cases, open-ended assessments can be used to test more complex reasoning, such as logical thinking, interpretation, or analysis.

The second type of constructed-response written assessment includes essays, problem-based examinations, and scenarios. These items are like open-ended questions, except that they typically extend the demands made on students to include more complex situations, more difficult reasoning, and higher levels of understanding. Essays are familiar to most educators; they are lengthy written responses that can be scored in terms of content and/or conventions. Problem-based examinations include mathematical word problems and more open-ended challenges based on real-life situations that require students to apply their knowledge and skills to new settings. For example, in KIRIS, groups of three or four twelfth-grade students were given a problem about a Pep Club fund-raising sale in which they were asked to analyze the data, present their findings in graphical form, and make a recommendation about whether the event should be continued in the future. Scenarios are similar to problem-based examinations, but the setting is described in greater detail and the problem may be less well formed, calling for greater creativity. An example is the scenario portion of C-TAP, which requires students

Table 4

Broad Categories of Assessment

	Response Type	
Category	Selected	Constructed
Written assessments		
Multiple choice, true-false, matching	✔	
Open ended		✔
Essay, problem based, scenario		✔
Performance tasks		✔
Senior projects (research paper, project, oral presentation)		✔
Portfolios		✔

Written Assessments

Written assessments are activities in which the student selects or composes a response to a prompt. In most cases, the prompt consists of printed materials (a brief question, a collection of historical documents, graphic or tabular material, or a combination of these). However, it may also be an object, an event, or an experience. Student responses are usually produced "on demand," i.e., the respondent does the writing at a specified time and within a fixed amount of time. These constraints contribute to standardization of testing conditions, which increases the comparability of results across students or groups (a theme that is explored later in Chapters Four and Five).

Rahn et al. (1995) distinguish three types of written assessment, one of which involves selected responses and two of which involve constructed responses. The first type is multiple-choice tests,[2] which are commonly used for gathering information about knowledge of facts or the ability to perform specific operations (as in arithmetic). For example, in the Laborers-AGC programs, factual knowledge of environmental hazards and handling procedures is measured using multiple-choice tests. The Oklahoma testing program uses multiple-choice tests of occupational skills and knowledge derived from statewide job analyses.

---

[2]Matching and true-false tests are also selected-response written assessments.

scoring; and clarification of directions for some activities. Candidates who complete the process find it extremely rewarding despite the substantial burdens. The board intends for the system to drive preservice and inservice training and even to influence state licensing standards.

Oklahoma Department of Vocational-Technical Education Competency-Based Testing Program

The Oklahoma competency-based testing program encompasses a range of multiple-choice and performance-based assessments for both secondary and postsecondary students. The Oklahoma Department of Vocational-Technical Education (Oklahoma Vo-Tech) developed and oversees these tests, which are used to certify students for employment, to improve instruction and student learning through competency-based curriculum and assessment, and to report program improvement and accountability data at the state level. Students are required to pass two local performance assessments, attain all locally identified competencies, and then pass a written multiple-choice test. The responsibility for establishing competencies, certifying mastery, and conducting performance assessments rests with individual programs, with the associated variation from site to site. The multiple-choice component of the program is administered centrally and standardized across sites. Criterion-referenced multiple-choice tests have been developed for 250 occupational titles categorized into fifty-five program areas. The tests measure occupation-specific knowledge and skills. State staff feel confident about the tests' content validity based on the strong employer input into the assessment system, but no formal validation research has been done. Schools and occupational programs use the state curriculum guides to different degrees, so instruction and testing are not always closely tied. Oklahoma has a long-standing tradition of centralization and political support for vocational education, which has translated into substantial state funding. Without this acceptance of centralized authority and this level of support, other states may be hard-pressed to follow Oklahoma's example.

ments, though employer evaluation of certified employees is already quite positive. Because the fund is a shared venture between labor and management, employers have immediate input if their needs are not being met. The Laborers-AGC model carries high operational costs because of the depth and breadth of its hands-on activities and the need for extensive space (e.g., to create mock hazard sites), expensive equipment, and supplies actually used on the job.

National Board for Professional Teaching Standards Certification Program

The National Board for Professional Teaching Standards (NBPTS) offers voluntary national certification to recognize highly accomplished K–12 teachers. Although NBPTS is the only case we studied that does not focus on student assessment, we included it because of the interesting alternative assessment strategies it employs and the lessons that can be learned about assessment for certification. The board aims "to establish high and rigorous standards for what teachers should know and be able to do, to certify teachers who meet those standards, and to advance other education reforms for the purpose of improving student learning in American schools" (NBPTS, 1989, p. iii). The standards and tasks by which candidates are judged were developed mainly by teachers. To obtain the NBPTS certificate, teachers must prepare an extensive portfolio demonstrating their preparation, classroom work, teaching strategies, and professional activities, and must participate in a day of performance activities at a regional assessment center. Standards committees (mostly teachers) used a multistage process to develop subject-matter standards, and assessment development laboratories created the initial assessments. Assessments are still being developed/tested for many of the categories (combining one of four grade levels with one of fourteen subjects);[1] in 1995–1996, NBPTS certification was available in two fields. Extensive reviews of validity, reliability, and other quality-related factors have, on the whole, produced positive results (Bond et al., 1994). Areas that need improvement include reduction of the costs of test development, administration, and

---

[1]Draft standards have been developed for vocational education teachers, but no work has yet been done to develop these assessments.

REFERENCES

American Psychological Association (1985). Standards for Educational and Psychological Testing. Washington, D.C.: American Psychological Association.

American Vocational Association (1992). *AVA Guide to the Carl D. Perkins Vocational and Applied Technology Education Act of 1990.* Updated edition. Alexandria, VA: American Vocational Association.

Baker, E. L. (1992). *The Role of Domain Specifications in Improving the Technical Quality of Performance Assessment.* Tech. Report. Los Angeles: University of California Center for Research on Evaluation, Standards, and Student Testing.

Bennett, R. E., and Sebrechts, M. M. (1996). "The Accuracy of Expert-System Diagnoses of Mathematical Problem Solutions." *Applied Measurement in Education,* 9(2), 133-150.

Berryman, S., and Bailey, T. (1992). *The Double Helis of Education and the Economy.* New York: Teachers College.

Bishop, J. (1995). "High School Training: When Does It Pay Off?" *Economics of Education Review,* 8(1), 1-15.

Boesel, D., and McFarland, L. (1994, July). *National Assessment of Vocational Education: Final Report to Congress.* Volume 1: Summary and Recommendations. Washington, D.C.: U.S. Department of Education.

Bond, L., and Linn, R. (1994). *An Analysis of Adverse Impact in Rates of Certification on the Early Adolescence/Generalist Assessment.* Greensboro, NC: Technical Analysis Group, National Board for Professional Teaching Standards.

Bond, L., Cronbach, L. J., Haertel, E., Jaeger, R. M., Linn, R. L., and Lloyd, B. (1994). *Conclusions on the Technical Measurement Quality of the National Board for Professional Teaching Standards' Early Adolescence Generalist Assessment.* Greensboro, NC: Technical Analysis Group, National Board for Professional Teaching Standards.

Bradley, A. (1994, April 20). "Pioneers in Professionalism." *Education Week.*

Bradley, A. (1995a, May 31). "Overruns Spur Teacher Board to Alter Plans." *Education Week.*

Bradley, A. (1995b, May 31). "Teacher Board Providing Valuable Lessons in Using Portfolios." *Education Week.*

Cape, W., Dickey, L., and Anderson, J. (1995). "Design Considerations for NBPTS Assessments." Paper presented at the annual meeting of the American Educational Research Association.

Carnegie Task Force on Technology as a Profession (1986). *A Nation Prepared: Teachers for the 21st Century.* New York: Carnegie Foundation.

Comfort, K. B. (1995, April). "The California Perspective." In B. Stecher (chair), "The Cost of Performance Assessment in Science." Symposium presented at the annual meeting of the National Council on Measurement in Education, San Francisco.

Doolittle, A. (1995, April). "The SCASS Perspective." In B. Stecher (chair), "The Cost of Performance Assessment in Science." Symposium presented at the annual meeting of the National Council on Measurement in Education, San Francisco.

Electronic Industries Association and Electronic Industries Foundation (1994). *Raising the Standard: Electronics Technician Skills for Today and Tomorrow.* Washington, D.C.: Electronic Industries Association and Electronic Industries Foundation.

Felkner, D. (1994). *A Formative Evaluation of Scorer Training for Early Adolescence Generalist Exercises.* Greensboro, NC: Technical Analysis Group, National Board for Professional Teaching Standards.

Gearhart, M., Herman, J. L., Baker, E. L., and Whittaker, A. K. (1993). *Whose Work Is It: A Question for the Validity of Large-Scale Portfolio Assessment.* CSE Tech. Report 363. Los Angeles: University of California Center for Research on Evaluation, Standards, and Student Testing.

Hambleton, R. K., Jaeger, R. M., Koretz, D., Linn, R. L., Millman, J., and Phillips, S. E. (1995). *Review of the Measurement Quality of the Kentucky Instructional Results Information System, 1991–1994.* Frankfort: Office of Educational Accountability, Kentucky General Assembly.

Hardy, R. (1995). "Examining the Cost of Performance Assessment." *Applied Measurement in Education,* 8(2), 121-134.

Hattie, J., Sackett, P., and Millman, J. (1994). *A Description and Evaluation of the NBPTS' Initial Process for Establishing Teacher Certification Standards, Second Draft.* Greensboro, NC: Technical Analysis Group, National Board for Professional Teaching Standards.

Heider, C., Herbert, J., Lashley, J., McLeod, R., Perry, J., and Strahan, D. *A Commissioned Study of the Application of the Early Adolescence Generalist Scoring System to 1993–1994 Early Adolescence Generalist Candidate Submissions.* Greensboro, NC: Technical Analysis Group, National Board for Professional Teaching Standards.

Herman, J. L., Aschbacher, P. R., and Winters, L. (1992). *A Practical Guide to Alternative Assessment.* Alexandria, VA: Association for Supervision and Curriculum Development.

Hill, C., and Larson, E. (1992, December). *Testing and Assessment in Secondary Education: A Critical Review of Emerging Practices.* Berkeley, CA: National Center for Research in Vocational Education.

Hoover, H. D., and Bray, G. B. (1995). "The Research and Development Phase: Can a Performance Assessment Be Cost-Effective?" Paper presented at the annual meeting of the American Educational Research Association, San Francisco.

Hunt, J. B. (1995, October 23). "A Course That Creates A+ Teachers." *USA Today*, p. 13A.

Jaeger, R. (1994)69*ards for the National Board for Professional Teaching Standards' Early Adolescence Generalist Assessment.* Greensboro, NC: Technical Analysis Group, National Board for Professional Teaching Standards.

Kentucky Department of Education (1993). *KIRIS: 1991–92 Technical Report.* Frankfort: Kentucky Department of Education.

Kentucky Department of Education (1995a). *KIRIS: 1992–93 Technical Report.* Frankfort: Kentucky Department of Education.

Kentucky Department of Education (1995b). *KIRIS Accountability Cycle I Technical Manual.* Frankfort: Kentucky Department of Education.

Kentucky Institute for Education Research (1994). *A Review of Research on the Kentucky Education Reform Act (KERA).* Frankfort: Kentucky Department of Education.

Kentucky Institute for Education Research (1995). *An Independent Evaluation of the Kentucky Instructional Results Information System (KIRIS).* Frankfort: Kentucky Department of Education.

Koretz, D., Linn, R., Dunbar, S., and Shepard, L. (1991). "The Effects of High Stakes Testing on Achievement." Presentation at the annual meeting of the American Educational Research Association, Chicago.

Koretz, D., Mitchell, K., Barron, S., and Stecher, B. (1996). *Perceived Effects of the Kentucky Instructional Results Information System (KIRIS).* MR-792-PCT/FF. Santa Monica, CA: RAND.

Koretz, D., Stecher, B., Klein, S., and McCaffrey, D. (1994, Fall). "The Vermont Portfolio Assessment Program: Findings and Implications." *Educational Measurement: Issues and Practice,* 13(3), 5-16.

Koretz, D., Stecher, B., Klein, S., McCaffrey, D., and Deibert, E. (1993, December). *Can Portfolios Assess Student Performance and Influence Instruction? The 1991–92 Vermont Experience.* CSE Tech. Report 371. Los Angeles: University of California Center for Research on Evaluation, Standards, and Student Testing. (Reprinted as RP-259, RAND, 1994.)

Lazerson, M., and Grubb, W. N. (1974). *American Education and Vocationalism: A Documentary History 1870–1970.* New York: Teachers College Press.

LeMahieu, P. (1993, April). "Data from the Pittsburgh Writing Portfolio Assessment." In J. Herman (chair), "Portfolio Assessment Meets the Reality of Data." Symposium presented at the annual meeting of the American Educational Research Association, Atlanta.

Levesque, K., Premo, M., Vergun, R., Emanuel, D., Klein, S., Henke, R., Kagehire, S., and Houser, J. (1995). *Vocational Education in the United States: The Early 1990s.* NCES 95-024. Washington, D.C.: U.S. Department of Education.

Linn, R. L. (1993). "Educational Assessment: Expanded Expectations and Challenges." *Educational Evaluation and Policy Analysis,* 15(1), 1-16.

Linn, R. L., Baker, E. L., and Dunbar, S. (1992). *Complex, Performance-Based Assessments: Expectations and Validation Criteria.* CSE Tech. Report 331. Los Angeles: University of California Center for Research on Evaluation, Standards, and Student Testing.

Lloyd, B., and Crocker, L. (No date). *Matching Exercises, Aspect Guides, and Decision Guides to Standards of the Early Adolescence/Generalist Certification Process: A Preliminary Content Validation.* Greensboro, NC: Technical Analysis Group, National Board for Professional Teaching Standards.

McDonnell, L. M. (1994). *Policymakers' Views of Student Assessment.* MR-348-UCLA/OERI. Santa Monica, CA: RAND.

Mehrens, W. (1992, Spring). "Using Performance Assessment for Accountability Purposes." *Educational Measurement: Issues and Practice,* 11(1), 3-20.

Messick, S. (1989). "Validity." In R. L. Linn (ed.), *Educational Measurement.* Third edition. New York: Macmillan.

Miller, M., and Legg, S. (1993, Summer). "Alternative Assessment in a High-Stakes Environment." *Educational Measurement: Issues and Practice,* 12(2), 9-15.

MPR Associates (1996). "Skill Standards: Concepts and Practice in State and Local Education." Unpublished. Berkeley, CA.

NBPTS (National Board for Professional Teaching Standards) (1989). *Toward High and Rigorous Standards for the Teaching Profession.*

NBPTS (1990a, April 11). "Request for Proposals for Award of Contract to Establish the First Assessment Development Laboratory for the Early Adolescence/English Language Arts Certificate."

NBPTS (1990b, July 16). "Request for Proposals for Award of Contract to Establish the Second Assessment Development Laboratory for the Early Adolescence/Generalist Certificate."

NBPTS (1991). "Draft Request for Proposals for Multiple Assessment Development Laboratories, RFP #6."

NBPTS (1992). "School Districts Join Nationwide Network in First Step Toward National Teacher Certification System." Press release.

NBPTS (1995). *An Invitation to National Board Certification.*

NBPTS, Executive Committee (1989). "Strategic Plan for the National Board for Professional Teaching Standards."

O'Neil, H. F., Jr., Allred, K., and Dennis, R. A. (1992). *Simulation as a Performance Assessment Technique for the Interpersonal Skill of Negotiation.* CSE Tech. Report 343. Los Angeles: University of California Center for Research on Evaluation, Standards, and Student Testing.

Rahn, M. L. (1995). *Emerging National Influences in Education Policy.* Doctoral Dissertation (unpublished). University of California at Berkeley.

Rahn, M. L., Alt, M., Emanuel, D., Ramer, C., Hoachlander, E. G., Holmes, P., Jackson, M., Klein, S., and Rossi, K. (1995, December). *Getting to Work: A Guide for Better Schools.* Berkeley, CA: MPR Associates.

Richardson, L. (1995, January 6). "First 81 Teachers Qualify for National Certification." *The New York Times,* p. A1.

Scriven, M. (1994). *Summary Report on the Administration of the Assessment Process for NBPTS.* Inverness, CA: Evaluation & Development Group.

Shavelson, R. J., Baxter, G. P., and Pine, J. (1992). "Performance Assessments: Political Rhetoric and Measurement Reality." *Educational Researcher,* 21(4), 22-27.

Shavelson, R. J., Gao, X., and Baxter, G. P. (1993). "Sampling Variability of Performance Assessments." *Journal of Educational Measurement,* 30, 215-232.

Shepard, L. (1991). "Will National Tests Improve Student Learning?" *Phi Delta Kappan,* 71, 232-238.

Shepard, L., and Dougherty, K. (1991). "Effects of High Stakes Testing on Instruction." Paper presented at the annual meeting of the American Educational Research Association and the National Council on Measurement in Education, New Orleans.

Smith, M. L., and Rottenberg, C. (1991). "Unintended Consequences of External Testing in Elementary Schools." *Educational Measurement: Issues and Practice,* 10(4), 7-11.

Stasz, C., Ramsey, K., Eden, R., Melamid, E., and Kaganoff, T. (1996). *Workplace Skills in Practice.* MR-722-NCRVE/UCB. Santa Monica, CA: RAND.

Stecher, B. M. (1995, April). "The RAND Perspective." In B. Stecher (chair), "The Cost of Performance Assessment in Science."

Symposium presented at the annual meeting of the National Council on Measurement in Education, San Francisco.

Stecher, B. M., and Herman, J. (1997). "Using Portfolios for Large-Scale Assessment." In G. D. Phye (ed.), *Handbook of Classroom Assessment*. San Diego: Academic Press.

Stecher, B. M., and Klein, S. P. (in press). "The Cost of Science Performance Assessment in Large-Scale Testing Programs." *Educational Evaluation and Policy Analysis*.

Traub, R. (1994a). *Report on a Study of Decision Consistency Based on Data from the 1993–1994 Field Test of the National Board for Professional Teaching Standards' Early Adolescence Generalist Assessment*. Report to the Technical Analysis Group, National Board for Professional Teaching Standards.

Traub, R. (1994b). *Report on a Study of the Generalizability of Scores Earned on the Seven Exercises of the National Board for Professional Teaching Standards' Early Adolescence Generalist Assessment Based on Data from the 1993–1994 Field Test*. Report to the Technical Analysis Group, National Board for Professional Teaching Standards.

U. S. Congress (1990, September 25). The Carl D. Perkins Vocational and Applied Technology Education Act. P.L. 101-392.

U. S. Congress, Office of Technology Assessment (1992). *Testing in American Schools: Asking the Right Questions*. Office of Technology Assessment.

Vocational Education Journal (1995, May). "Data File: Vocational Education by the Numbers." 70(5), 28-31.

Wiggins, G. (1989, May). "A True Test: Toward More Authentic and Equitable Assessment." *Phi Delta Kappan*, 70(9), 703-713.

Wirt, J. G. (1995). *Performance Assessment Systems: Implications for a National System of Skill Standards*. Volume II—Technical Report. Washington, D. C.: National Governors' Association.

Wolf, D. P. (1992, May). "Good Measures: Assessment as a Tool for Educational Reform." *Educational Leadership*, 49(8), 8-13.